TOP
100
PASTA DISHES

TOP
100
PASTA DISHES

SAFEWAY/GOOD HOUSEKEEPING

Published exclusively for
Safeway
6 Millington Road, Hayes, Middlesex UB3 4AY
by Ebury Press
A division of Random House
20 Vauxhall Bridge Road
London SW1V 2SA

First published 1993

Edited by Felicity Jackson and Beverly LeBlanc
Designed by Peartree Design Associates
Special photography by Ken Field
Food stylist Kerenza Harries
Photographic stylists Sue Russell and Suzy Gittins

The paper in this book is acid-free

Typeset by Textype Typesetters, Cambridge
Printed in Italy

ISBN 0 09 182101 0

COOKERY NOTES

All spoon measures are level unless otherwise stated.

Size 2 eggs should be used except when otherwise stated.

Granulated sugar is used unless otherwise stated.

The oven should be preheated to the required
temperature unless otherwise stated.

Contents

FOREWORD

TOP 100 PASTA DISHES is one of a popular new series of colourful and practical cookery books created exclusively for Safeway customers. It contains a selection of delicious *Good Housekeeping* pasta recipes.

The Good Housekeeping Institute is unique in the field of food and cookery, and every recipe has been created and double-tested in the Institute's world-famous kitchens.

Perfect for today's lifestyle, the recipes include soups and starters, meat, fish and vegetarian main courses, plus an imaginative choice of pasta salads.

COOKERY EDITOR
GOOD HOUSEKEEPING

CHICKEN AND PASTA BROTH

SERVES 6

2 × 275 g (10 oz) chicken portions, skin removed
1-2 small leeks, trimmed, sliced and washed
2 carrots, peeled and thinly sliced
900 ml (1½ pt) chicken stock
900 ml (1½ pt) water
1 bouquet garni
salt and freshly ground black pepper
50 g (2 oz) small dried pasta shapes, such as
   spirals or shells
chopped fresh parsley, to garnish

1. Put the chicken portions in a large saucepan with the sliced leeks and carrots. Pour in the chicken stock and water and bring to the boil.
2. Add the bouquet garni and salt and pepper to taste, then lower the heat, cover the pan and simmer for 30 minutes until the chicken is tender.
3. Remove the chicken from the liquid using a slotted spoon and leave until cool enough to handle.
4. Meanwhile, place the pasta in the pan of liquid and return to the boil. Cook for 10-12 minutes, stirring occasionally, or until the pasta is just tender.
5. Remove the chicken flesh from the bones and cut the flesh into bite-sized pieces.
6. Return the chicken to the pan and heat through. Discard the bouquet garni and taste and adjust seasoning. Serve hot in warmed soup bowls, with each portion sprinkled with a little chopped parsley.

Chicken and Pasta Broth

PASTA SHAPES IN BEEF STOCK

SERVES 6

1.5 lt (2½ pt) beef stock
400 g (14 oz) medium-sized dried pasta shapes,
    such as spirals or shells
salt and freshly ground black pepper
freshly grated Parmesan cheese, to serve

I. In a large saucepan, bring the beef stock to the boil.
2. Add the pasta and return to the boil. Cook for 10-12 minutes, or until just tender.
3. Season to taste, then pour into six warmed soup bowls. Serve immediately with freshly grated Parmesan cheese handed around separately.

VARIATION This light, refreshing soup is equally good if made with chicken stock.

HOME-MADE PASTA DOUGH

MAKES ABOUT 335 G (12 OZ) DOUGH

about 200 g (7 oz) strong white flour
2 eggs, beaten
pinch of salt
I × 15 ml tbs olive oil

I. Sift the flour into a mound on a clean working surface and make a well in the centre. Add the eggs, salt, and oil.
2. Using your fingertips, gradually draw the flour into the eggs. Continue until the dough comes together.
3. Then, using both hands, knead the dough on a lightly floured surface for about 10 minutes until smooth and not sticky.
4. Form the dough into a ball, place in a polythene bag and leave to rest for 30 minutes before shaping as required.

VARIATIONS
Spinach Pasta Wash, drain and discard the coarse stalks from 225 g (8 oz) fresh spinach. Cook in a saucepan, with just the water that clings to the leaves, until tender. Cool, then squeeze out all the excess moisture. Finely chop the spinach. Increase the flour in the dough to 225 g (8 oz) and add the spinach to the mixture with the eggs.

Red Pasta Skin 1 medium red pepper, then purée in a blender or food processor. Add to the flour with the eggs and oil, increasing the flour to 225 g (8 oz).

Herb Pasta Add 2 × 15 ml tbs chopped fresh basil or parsley to the flour with the eggs and oil.

SHAPING DOUGH
If using a pasta machine, put your dough through on the chosen setting, sprinkling very lightly with flour if it is becomes sticky.

Alternatively, roll out the pasta on a floured work surface to a large rectangle which is nearly paper thin. If you are making cut pasta, such as tagliatelle or fettucine, the dough must be allowed to dry. Place the dough on a clean tea towel, allowing one third to hang over the edge of a table or work surface and turn every 10 minutes. The pasta is ready to cut when it is dry to the touch, about 30 minutes. Lightly fold the dough over into a roll about 7.5 cm (3 in) in depth. Cut into 1 cm (½ in) wide strips for tagliatelle, or 0.6 cm (¼ in) wide strips for fettucine. For a fluted edge, cut one or both sides with a pasta wheel. Unfold and leave to dry for about 10 minutes.

MINESTRONE

SERVES 6–8

175 g (6 oz) dried cannellini beans, soaked
  overnight in cold water
4 × 15 ml tbs olive oil
2 onions, skinned and chopped
3 garlic cloves, skinned and crushed
2 carrots, peeled and diced
2 celery sticks, washed and diced
400 g can chopped tomatoes
2.4 lt (4 pt) vegetable stock
335 g (12 oz) floury potatoes, such as King Edward
  or Maris Piper, peeled and diced
115 g (4 oz) small dried pasta shapes
115 g (4 oz) shelled fresh or frozen peas
175 g (6 oz) French beans, topped, tailed and sliced
225 g (8 oz) dark green cabbage, tough stalks
  removed and roughly chopped
5 × 15 ml tbs chopped fresh parsley
4 × 15 ml tbs pesto sauce
salt and freshly ground black pepper
extra pesto and freshly grated Parmesan cheese

1. Drain the beans. Put them in a very large saucepan and cover with fresh water. Bring to the boil and boil rapidly for 10 minutes, then cover and simmer for 1 hour. Drain well.
2. Meanwhile, heat the oil in a large saucepan and fry the onions and garlic for 5-10 minutes until golden. Add the carrots and celery and fry for 2 minutes, stirring occasionally.
3. Stir in the beans, tomatoes, stock, potatoes, pasta and fresh peas, if using. Bring to the boil, then half-cover and simmer for 1 hour.
4. Stir in the frozen peas, if using, French beans, cabbage, parsley and pesto sauce. Season with salt and pepper and simmer for 30 minutes, or until the vegetables are tender.
5. Serve immediately in a warmed soup tureen, with the extra pesto and cheese in separate bowls for guests to stir into their soup.

COOK'S TIP This traditional Italian soup is hearty enough to be a main course, simply served with chunks of Italian bread.

Minestrone

Spaghetti alla Carbonara

SERVES 4

2 × 15 ml tbs olive oil
1 onion, skinned and finely chopped
1 garlic clove, skinned and crushed
400 g (14 oz) dried spaghetti
salt and freshly ground black pepper
6 rashers of unsmoked streaky bacon, rinded and
   cut into thin strips
4 × 15 ml tbs dry white wine
150 ml (5 fl oz) double cream
4 × 15 ml tbs freshly grated Parmesan cheese
2 × 15 ml tbs chopped fresh parsley

1. Heat the oil in a frying pan and fry the onion for 5 minutes, stirring occasionally, until soft but not coloured. Add the garlic and fry for 1 minute further.
2. Cook the spaghetti in boiling salted water for 10–12 minutes, or until just tender.
3. Meanwhile, add the bacon to the onion and fry for 2 minutes over high heat, stirring occasionally. Add the wine, and boil until evaporated.
4. In a bowl, mix together the cream, Parmesan cheese, parsley and salt and pepper to taste.
5. Drain the spaghetti. Return to the pan with the bacon and onion mixture. Mix well over moderate heat for 1 minute.
6. Remove from the heat and pour in the cream mixture, mixing well. The heat from the spaghetti will heat the cream. Place in a warmed serving dish and serve immediately.

VARIATION For a vegetarian alternative, replace the streaky bacon with 225 g (8 oz) button mushrooms, halved, and fried with the onion until just wilted.

Parsleyed Linguine with Smoked Salmon

SERVES 8

450 g (1 lb) dried linguine pasta
1 × 15 ml tbs vegetable oil
salt and freshly ground black pepper
75 g (3 oz) unsalted butter
1 garlic clove, skinned and crushed
3-4 × 15 ml tbs chopped fresh parsley
2 × 15 ml tbs lemon juice
198 g can mussels in vinegar, drained and rinsed
225 g (8 oz) thinly sliced smoked salmon, cut into
   thin strips
1-2 × 15 ml tbs grated Parmesan cheese
fresh parsley or coriander, to garnish

1. Place the pasta and oil in a large saucepan of boiling salted water and return to the boil. Cook for 10–12 minutes, or until just tender. Drain well.
2. Melt the butter in a large frying pan. Add the garlic, parsley and drained pasta and toss together for 1 minute.
3. Add the lemon juice and pepper (do not add any salt), then stir in the mussels and smoked salmon and toss over a medium heat for 1–2 minutes, or until heated through.
4. Sprinkle with the Parmesan cheese and serve immediately, garnished with parsley or coriander.

COOK'S TIP Linguine are very thin, flat noodles. If you cannot find any, substitute spaghetti. For extra colour, you can use a mixture of spinach and plain egg linguine.

Parsleyed Linguine with Smoked Salmon

TAGLIATELLE WITH GORGONZOLA SAUCE

SERVES 4

25 g (1 oz) butter
175 g (6 oz) Gorgonzola cheese
150 ml (5 fl oz) whipping cream
2 × 15 ml tbs dry white wine
1 × 15 ml tbs chopped fresh sage
salt and freshly ground black pepper
335 g (12 oz) dried tagliatelle or other noodles

1. Melt the butter in a heavy-based saucepan. Crumble in the Gorgonzola cheese, then stir over a gentle heat for 2-3 minutes until the cheese has melted.
2. Pour in the cream and wine, whisking vigorously. Stir in the sage, season to taste with salt and freshly ground black pepper and cook, stirring, until the sauce thickens. Remove the pan from the heat.
3. Cook the tagliatelle in boiling salted water for 10-12 minutes, or until just tender. Drain thoroughly.
4. Gently reheat the Gorgonzola sauce, whisking vigorously all the time. Taste and adjust seasoning.
5. Divide the tagliatelle equally between four warmed serving bowls. Top each portion with sauce and serve immediately.

13

FRESH RAVIOLI

SERVES 4

335 g (12 oz) fresh spinach, trimmed and washed
    or 175 g (6 oz) frozen spinach
175 g (6 oz) ricotta or curd cheese
115 g (4 oz) Parmesan cheese, freshly grated
1 egg, beaten
pinch of freshly grated nutmeg or ground allspice
salt and freshly ground black pepper
Home-made Pasta Dough made with 3 eggs and
    300 g (11 oz) strong white flour (see page 10)
1 egg, beaten, or water, for glazing
75 g (3 oz) butter
a few fresh sage leaves, chopped, and a few extra,
    to garnish

1. Place the spinach in a saucepan without any water and cook gently for 5–10 minutes, or until thawed if using frozen spinach. Drain very well and chop the spinach finely.
2. Mix together the spinach, ricotta or curd cheese, 65 g (2½ oz) of the Parmesan cheese, the egg, nutmeg or allspice and seasoning.
3. Cut the dough in two. Wrap one half in clingfilm. Pat the other half out to a rectangle, then roll out firmly to an even sheet of almost paper-thin pasta. If it sticks, ease it carefully and flour underneath. Make sure there are no holes or creases. Cover with a clean damp cloth and repeat with other half of dough.
4. Working quickly to prevent the pasta drying out, place teaspoonfuls of filling at 4 cm (1½ in) intervals across and down the sheet of dough that has just been rolled out.
5. With a pastry brush or finger, glaze the spaces between the filling with the beaten egg or water. This acts as a bond to seal the ravioli.
6. Uncover the other sheet of pasta, carefully lift this on the rolling pin and unroll it over the first sheet. Press down firmly around the pockets of filling and along the dampened lines to push out any trapped air and seal well.
7. With a ravioli cutter, serrated-edged wheel or a sharp knife, cut the ravioli into squares between the pouches. Lift the ravioli one by one on to a well-floured baking tray and leave to dry for about 1 hour before cooking. Or cover with clingfilm and refrigerate overnight.
8. Bring a large saucepan of lightly salted water to the boil. Add a few ravioli at a time and return to the boil. Cook for about 3–5 minutes, or until just tender.
9. Remove with a slotted spoon and place in a warmed buttered serving dish. Keep hot while cooking the remainder of the ravioli.
10. Melt the butter in a saucepan and stir in the rest of the grated Parmesan cheese with the chopped sage. Pour over the ravioli and toss to coat evenly. Serve immediately, garnished with fresh sage.

PASTA SHELLS WITH CHEESE AND WALNUTS

SERVES 4

275 g (10 oz) dried pasta shells or other shapes
salt and freshly ground black pepper
25 g (1 oz) butter
250 g packet mascarpone cheese, or other full-fat
    soft cheese
2 × 15 ml tbs freshly grated Parmesan cheese
75 g (3 oz) walnuts, roughly chopped

1. Cook the pasta shells in boiling salted water for 15–20 minutes, or until just tender.
2. In another pan, melt the butter. Add the mascarpone cheese and stir for 2–3 minutes until heated through. Do not boil.
3. Add the Parmesan cheese and walnuts and stir together. Drain the pasta well and add to the cheese mixture. Mix well until evenly coated with sauce. Season to taste. Serve immediately.

Pasta Shells with Cheese and Walnuts

QUICK AND EASY PASTA SAUCES

TOMATO SAUCE

SERVES 4

2 × 15 ml tbs olive oil
1 small onion, skinned and finely chopped
2 × 15 ml tbs tomato purée
1 × 5 ml tsp mild paprika
2 × 400 g cans chopped tomatoes
large pinch of dried oregano
300 ml (10 fl oz) dry red wine or vegetable stock
large pinch of sugar
salt and freshly ground black pepper

1. Heat the oil in a saucepan, add the onion and fry for 5–10 minutes or until soft. Add the purée and paprika. Fry for 2–3 minutes. Add the tomatoes, oregano, wine or stock, and sugar.
2. Season with salt and pepper, then bring to the boil and simmer, uncovered, for about 20 minutes or until the sauce is slightly reduced.

VARIATION Add 1-2 chopped fresh chillies and a little chopped fresh coriander.

TOASTED GARLIC CRUMBS

SERVES 4

2 × 15 ml tbs olive oil
2 garlic cloves, skinned and crushed
75 g (3 oz) fine fresh white breadcrumbs
salt and freshly ground black pepper
3 × 15 ml tbs chopped fresh chives or parsley

Heat the oil in a large frying pan and fry the garlic and breadcrumbs over a medium heat, stirring, for 3–4 minutes until golden. Add a little more oil if necessary. Season and stir in the chopped herbs. Serve as an accompaniment to any of the sauces that follow.

Hazelnut and Coriander Pesto, see page 20 (left)
Tomato Sauce (right)

GARLIC AND OIL SAUCE

SERVES 4

8 × 15 ml tbs olive oil
2 garlic cloves, skinned and finely chopped
salt and freshly ground black pepper

1. Place the oil, garlic and seasoning in a small saucepan and fry very gently, stirring all the time, for 2-3 minutes until the garlic is golden.
2. Pour over freshly cooked pasta, and toss together before serving.

SWEET TOMATO SAUCE

SERVES 4

2 × 15 ml tbs olive oil
115 g (4 oz) onion, skinned and finely chopped
1 garlic clove, skinned and crushed
175 g (6 oz) green pepper, seeded and
    roughly chopped
2 × 400 g cans tomatoes
¼ × 5 ml tsp mild chilli powder
2 × 5 ml tsp sugar
1 × 5 ml tsp made English mustard
1 × 5 ml tsp lemon juice
salt and freshly ground black pepper
2 × 15 ml tbs chopped fresh parsley

1. Heat the olive oil in a large saucepan and fry the onion and garlic for about 5 minutes until soft and golden.
2. Stir in the green pepper and cook for 2-3 minutes, stirring, until softened.
3. In a blender or food processor, purée all the remaining ingredients, except the parsley.
4. Stir the puréed tomato mix into the onion and pepper mixture. Bring to the boil, then simmer gently for about 30 minutes, uncovered, until the mixture becomes slightly thickened.
5. Season and stir in the parsley to serve.

CLASSIC TOMATO SAUCE

SERVES 4

1 × 15 ml tbs olive oil
75 g (3 oz) onion, skinned and chopped
75 g (3 oz) celery, trimmed and chopped
75 g (3 oz) carrot, peeled and chopped
50 g (2 oz) sun-dried tomatoes in olive oil, drained
    weight, finely chopped
1 garlic clove, skinned and crushed
2 × 400 g cans chopped tomatoes
2 × 15 ml tbs tomato purée
150 ml (5 fl oz) vegetable or chicken stock
115 ml (4 fl oz) dry red wine
salt and freshly ground black pepper
Parmesan cheese, to serve

1. Heat the olive oil in a large saucepan. Add the vegetables, except the sun-dried tomatoes, and add the garlic. Cook, stirring continuously, for 5 minutes or until beginning to soften but not colour.
2. Stir in the canned tomatoes, tomato purée, stock, wine and seasoning. Simmer, covered, for about 30 minutes, stirring occasionally.
3. In a blender or food processor, purée the sauce, then stir in the sun-dried tomatoes.
4. Adjust seasoning and reheat to serve before pouring the sauce over hot pasta. Top with shavings of Parmesan cheese.

VARIATIONS
Chilli Tomato Sauce Add 1 small, finely chopped red chilli in step 1.

Mushroom and Parsley Sauce Add 115 g (4 oz) wiped and thinly sliced brown cap mushrooms and 2 × 15 ml tbs chopped fresh parsley when reheating the sauce.

Classic Tomato Sauce

HAZELNUT AND CORIANDER PESTO

SERVES 4–6

75 g (3 oz) shelled hazelnuts, with skins on
1 large bunch of coriander, weighing about 115 g
    (4 oz), stalks removed
2-3 garlic cloves, skinned and crushed
finely grated rind and juice of ½ lemon
about 150 ml (5 fl oz) olive oil
salt and freshly ground black pepper

1. Toast the hazelnuts under a hot grill. Tip them on to a clean tea towel and rub off the loose skins. Toast again under the grill until golden on all sides. Leave to cool, then tip into a blender or food processor.
2. Put the coriander leaves into the blender or food processor with the hazelnuts. Add the garlic and the lemon rind and juice. Process until finely chopped.
3. With the machine still running, gradually add the oil in a thin, steady stream, as if making mayonnaise, until you have a fairly thick sauce-like consistency.
4. Season with black pepper and a little salt. Store for up to 2 weeks in a screw-topped jar in the refrigerator. To serve, adjust the seasoning and toss with freshly cooked pasta.

COOK'S TIP This makes a vibrant green pesto with a pungent smell and a strong flavour. Serve it separately for guests to mix to taste with their individual plates of steaming pasta, dilute it with fromage frais or yogurt and toss with cooked vegetables and pulses.

CREAM SAUCE

SERVES 4

25 g (1 oz) butter
300 ml (10 fl oz) double cream
salt and freshly ground black pepper
25 g (1 oz) Parmesan cheese, freshly grated, plus
    extra for serving
freshly cooked pasta, to serve

1. Melt the butter in a saucepan. Pour in the cream and bring to the boil, then cook for 2-3 minutes, stirring constantly, until slightly thickened. Add the seasoning.
2. Stir in the Parmesan and serve over freshly cooked pasta. Sprinkle with extra cheese.

GORGONZOLA AND ROSEMARY SAUCE

SERVES 4

200 ml (7 fl oz) single cream
115 g (4 oz) Gorgonzola cheese, or other creamy
    blue cheese such as Cambozola, roughly
    chopped
50 g (2 oz) Edam cheese, roughly chopped
1 × 15 ml tbs chopped fresh rosemary
4 × 15 ml tbs water
freshly ground black pepper
freshly cooked pasta, to serve
rosemary sprigs, to garnish (optional)

1. Put the cream, half of both cheeses and the rosemary into a small saucepan. Heat gently until the cheese has melted, stirring.
2. Add the water, and bring to the boil. Stir in the remaining cheeses until melted. Season with pepper and serve with freshly cooked pasta, garnished with rosemary, if wished.

Gorgonzola and Rosemary Sauce

LENTIL AND TOMATO SAUCE

SERVES 3–4

2 × 15 ml tbs olive oil
225 g (8 oz) onion, skinned and chopped
1 garlic clove, skinned and chopped
115 g (4 oz) red lentils, rinsed and drained
150 ml (5 fl oz) vegetable stock
400 g can chopped tomatoes
150 g (5 oz) mushrooms, wiped and quartered
1 green pepper, seeded and sliced
salt and freshly ground black pepper
freshly cooked pasta, to serve
Gruyère cheese, grated, to serve

1. Heat the oil in a medium saucepan and fry the chopped onions and garlic for 2–3 minutes until soft but not coloured.

2. Rapidly boil the lentils in a saucepan for 10 minutes, then drain and add to the onion and garlic mix. Stir until the lentils are completely coated in oil.

3. Add the stock, tomatoes, mushrooms, green pepper and seasoning. Bring to the boil, then cover and simmer the sauce gently for about 30 minutes or until the red lentils are thoroughly softened.

4. Serve with freshly cooked pasta. Top with Gruyère cheese just before serving.

21

Vegetarian Bolognese Sauce

SERVES 8

2 × 15 ml tbs olive oil
1 celery stick, washed and finely chopped
2 carrots, peeled and finely chopped
1 onion, skinned and finely chopped
115 g (4 oz) mushrooms, wiped and finely chopped
2 garlic cloves, skinned and crushed
3 × 15 ml tbs tomato purée
2 × 400 g cans chopped tomatoes
300 ml (10 fl oz) dry red wine
600 ml (20 fl oz) vegetable stock
1 bay leaf
1 bouquet garni
1 × 5 ml tsp yeast extract savoury spread
1 × 5 ml tsp sugar
salt and freshly ground black pepper
freshly grated nutmeg
1 cinnamon stick
175 g (6 oz) soya mince, dried weight
3 × 15 ml tbs chopped fresh parsley
freshly cooked pasta, to serve

1. Heat the oil in a large, heavy-based saucepan and fry the celery, carrots, onion, mushrooms and garlic for about 5 minutes, or until softened.
2. Add the tomato purée and fry for 1 minute, then add all the remaining ingredients, except the parsley.
3. Bring to the boil, then reduce the heat, cover and simmer gently for 30-45 minutes, or until the soya mince is very tender.
4. Stir in the parsley and season with more salt, pepper and nutmeg, if necessary. Remove the cinnamon stick, bay leaf and bouquet garni and serve with freshly cooked pasta.

VARIATION To make a spicy version, add 1-2 fresh chopped green chillies instead of the bay leaf and bouquet garni.

Simple Meat Sauce

SERVES 12

3 × 15 ml tbs oil
450 g (1 lb) onions, skinned and chopped
2 garlic cloves, skinned and crushed
1.4 kg (3 lb) minced beef
6 × 15 ml tbs plain flour
3 × 400 g cans of chopped tomatoes
1 × 15 ml tbs tomato purée
600 ml (20 fl oz) beef stock
1 × 15 ml tbs dried mixed herbs
2 bay leaves
salt and freshly ground black pepper
freshly cooked pasta, to serve

1. Heat the oil in a large saucepan or flameproof casserole and fry the onions and garlic, stirring, for about 5 minutes until beginning to soften but not brown.
2. Add the minced beef and fry for 4-5 minutes, stirring occasionally to break up the minced beef.
3. Stir in the flour and cook, stirring, for 1-2 minutes. Add the remaining ingredients.
4. Bring to the boil, then cover and simmer gently for about 1 hour, stirring occasionally. Top up with stock if necessary. Adjust seasoning, remove the bay leaves and serve with freshly cooked pasta.

COOK'S TIP Cool, pack and freeze in family portions. To use: thaw overnight at cool room temperature, bring to the boil and simmer for 10-12 minutes.

VARIATION Add 1 celery stick, finely chopped, to the onions. Substitute white wine for 150 ml (5 fl oz) of the stock.

Vegetarian Bolognese Sauce

Sausage and Roasted Tomato Sauce

SERVES 4

450 g (1 lb) tomatoes, halved
2 × 15 ml tbs oil
115 g (4 oz) onion, skinned and chopped
2 × 5 ml tsp dried oregano
1 garlic clove, skinned and crushed
450 g (1 lb) pork sausages, skinned if
  preferred and thickly sliced
1 × 15 ml tbs tomato purée
salt and freshly ground black pepper
Tabasco sauce, to taste
freshly cooked pasta, to serve

1. Scoop the seeds out of the tomatoes into a sieve over a small bowl. Press the seeds with a wooden spoon to extract all the juice. Reserve.
2. Place the tomatoes, skin side up, under a hot grill and cook until well browned and blistered. Rub to remove the skins and roughly chop the flesh.
3. Heat the oil in a large saucepan and fry the onion, oregano and garlic for 2-3 minutes until beginning to soften. Add the sausages and continue to cook over a high heat, stirring, until well browned.
4. Stir in the tomatoes, reserved tomato juice, tomato purée, seasoning and Tabasco sauce. Bring to the boil, then reduce the heat and simmer gently, covered, for 10-12 minutes. Adjust the seasoning and serve over freshly cooked pasta.

COOK'S TIP Use a 400 g can chopped tomatoes instead of fresh ones for a quick alternative to this dish.

Tuna Fish Sauce

SERVES 4

200 g can tuna steaks in brine, drained and flaked
227 g can tomatoes
1 × 15 ml tbs chopped fresh parsley
salt and freshly ground black pepper
freshly cooked pasta, to serve

1. Place all the ingredients in a large saucepan, including the tomato juices. Break up the tomatoes with a wooden spoon and then bring to the boil, stirring.
2. Lower the heat and simmer, uncovered, for 5 minutes or until hot. Adjust the seasoning and serve over freshly cooked pasta. Toss together before serving.

Leek, Bacon and Cream Cheese Sauce

SERVES 4

25 g (1 oz) butter or margarine
225 g (8 oz) mushrooms, wiped and thinly sliced
115 g (4 oz) leeks, trimmed, sliced and washed
115 g (4 oz) streaky bacon, rinded and
  roughly chopped
1 garlic clove, skinned and crushed
115 g (4 oz) low-fat soft cheese with garlic
  and herbs
2 × 15 ml tbs milk or single cream
salt and freshly ground black pepper
freshly cooked pasta, to serve

1. In a medium saucepan, melt the butter and fry the mushrooms, leeks, bacon and garlic for 3-4 minutes or until the leeks are tender but still retain some bite.
2. Reduce the heat and stir in the cheese and milk until thoroughly mixed. Season.
3. Serve over freshly cooked pasta.

WALNUT AND BACON SAUCE

SERVES 4

50 ml (2 fl oz) olive oil
275 g (10 oz) smoked back bacon, rinded and
  chopped
1 garlic clove, skinned and crushed
75 g (3 oz) walnut pieces, chopped
450 g (1 lb) tomatoes, skinned and chopped
4 × 15 ml tbs chopped fresh parsley
grated rind of 1 lemon
freshly ground black pepper
225 (8 oz) soft cheese, such as goat's cheese or
  cheese with herbs and garlic, to serve (optional)
freshly cooked pasta, to serve

1. Heat the oil in a large frying pan and fry the bacon, garlic and walnuts together until golden, stirring occasionally.
2. Stir in the tomatoes, parsley, and grated lemon rind. Heat, stirring, for 1–2 minutes, or until piping hot. Season with black pepper.
3. Toss the walnut and bacon sauce with freshly cooked pasta. Serve immediately, topping each portion with pieces of soft cheese, if you like.

VARIATION Fry 1–2 shallots, cut into segments, with the bacon, garlic and walnuts. Serve the pasta garnished with sprigs of parsley.

Walnut and Bacon Sauce

TRADITIONAL BOLOGNESE SAUCE

SERVES 4

25 g (1 oz) butter or margarine
3 × 15 ml tbs olive oil
2 slices of unsmoked streaky bacon, rinded and
  finely chopped
225 g (8 oz) minced beef
1 small onion, skinned and finely chopped
1 small carrot, peeled and finely chopped
1 small celery stick, finely chopped
1 garlic clove, skinned and finely chopped
1 bay leaf
1 × 15 ml tbs tomato purée
150 ml (5 fl oz) dry white wine
150 ml (5 fl oz) beef stock
salt and freshly ground black pepper
freshly cooked pasta, to serve

1. Melt the butter with the oil in a saucepan, add the bacon and cook for 2-3 minutes until soft.
2. Add the minced beef and cook for a further 5 minutes, until lightly browned.
3. Add the onion, carrot, celery, garlic and bay leaf. Stir and cook for 2 minutes. Add the tomato purée, wine, stock and salt and pepper.
4. Bring to the boil, then simmer, for 1-1½ hours, stirring occasionally. Serve over freshly cooked pasta.

COOK'S TIP Spaghetti Bolognese makes a filling main course for a family meal or informal supper party. Serve with freshly grated Parmesan cheese, Italian red wine and a green salad tossed in olive oil and lemon juice.

Although originally from Bologna in northern Italy, Spaghetti Bolognese is now made all over the world, with literally hundreds of different variations. Streaky bacon is used in this version, but Italians would use pancetta, salted raw belly of pork.

CHICKEN AND BACON SAUCE

SERVES 4

225 g (8 oz) chicken livers, trimmed
335 g (12 oz) skinless chicken
  breast fillets
200 g (7 oz) back bacon
2 × 15 ml tbs oil
2 garlic cloves, skinned and crushed
400 g can chopped tomatoes
150 ml (5 fl oz) chicken stock
1 × 15 ml tbs sherry
1 × 15 ml tbs chopped fresh rosemary or
  ½ × 5 ml tsp dried rosemary
salt and freshly ground black pepper
12 stoned mixed olives (optional)
chopped fresh parsley and rosemary,
  to garnish
freshly cooked pasta, to serve

1. Roughly chop the chicken livers, fillets and bacon into bite-sized pieces.
2. Heat the oil in a large frying pan. Add the chicken, bacon and garlic and cook for about 5 minutes or until golden.
3. Add the tomatoes with the stock, sherry and rosemary and season to taste. Bring to the boil and simmer for 2-3 minutes.
4. Stir in the chicken livers with the olives, if using. Cook gently for a further 4-5 minutes, or until the chicken livers are tender and the sauce has thickened slightly. Add the sauce to the hot pasta and toss thoroughly to blend. Serve garnished with parsley and rosemary.

Chicken and Bacon Sauce

SPAGHETTI WITH RATATOUILLE SAUCE

SERVES 4

1 aubergine, diced
salt and freshly ground black pepper
1 onion, skinned and finely chopped
1 garlic clove, skinned and crushed
1 red pepper, seeded and cut into thin strips
3 medium courgettes, thinly sliced
335 g (12 oz) tomatoes, skinned and finely sliced
2 × 5 ml tsp chopped fresh basil
500 g wholewheat spaghetti
fresh basil, to garnish
freshly grated Parmesan cheese, to serve

1. Spread out the aubergine on a plate and sprinkle with salt. Leave for 20 minutes to remove the bitter flavour.
2. Tip the aubergine into a sieve and rinse under cold running water. Put into a large, heavy-based pan with the onion, garlic, pepper, courgettes, tomatoes, basil and salt and pepper to taste.
3. Cover and cook over moderate heat for 30 minutes, shaking the pan and stirring the vegetables frequently to encourage the juices to flow.
4. Meanwhile, cook the spaghetti in boiling salted water for 10-12 minutes, or until just tender. Drain well.
5. Place the spaghetti in a warmed serving dish. Taste and adjust the seasoning of the ratatouille sauce, then pour it over the spaghetti. Garnish with basil and serve immediately, with the Parmesan cheese handed separately.

Spaghetti with Ratatouille Sauce

Spaghetti with Butter and Parmesan

SERVES 4 AS A STARTER

225-335 g (8-12 oz) dried spaghetti
salt
50 g (2 oz) butter or margarine
50 g (2 oz) Parmesan cheese, freshly grated

1. Cook the spaghetti in boiling salted water for about 10-12 minutes, or until just tender.
2. Drain well and return to the pan. Add the butter and 15 g (½ oz) of Parmesan cheese. Stir and leave for a few minutes for the butter and cheese to melt. Serve with the remaining cheese in a separate dish.

VARIATION Add lightly cooked vegetables, such as broccoli or asparagus.

Pasta with Mushroom and Houmous Sauce

SERVES 2–3

50 g (2 oz) butter or margarine
225 g (8 oz) button mushrooms, wiped and sliced
1 bunch of salad onions, chopped
pinch of cumin seeds (optional)
225 g (8 oz) houmous
2 × 15 ml tbs milk
225 g (8 oz) dried spaghetti or tortellini
salt and freshly ground black pepper

1. Melt the butter in a medium saucepan and cook the mushrooms, onions and cumin seeds, stirring, for 2-3 minutes, or until the vegetables begin to soften.
2. Stir in the houmous and milk. Cover and simmer very gently for 5-10 minutes until the vegetables are tender.

3. Meanwhile, cook the pasta in boiling salted water for 10-12 minutes, or until just tender. Drain well.
4. Stir the pasta into the hot mushroom and houmous sauce. Add the seasoning and serve.

COOK'S TIP For a creamier sauce, add 2 × 15 ml tbs single cream to the hot mushroom and houmous sauce before stirring in the pasta.

Spring Vegetable Pasta

SERVES 4

115 g (4 oz) fresh asparagus or French beans, trimmed and cut into 5 cm (2 in) lengths
225 g (8 oz) leeks, trimmed, thinly sliced and washed
salt and freshly ground black pepper
175 g (6 oz) goat's cheese or full-fat soft cheese with garlic and herbs
150 g (5 oz) mascarpone cheese or 150 ml (5 fl oz) extra-thick double cream
50 g (2 oz) butter or margarine
2 × 15 ml tbs olive oil
1 onion, skinned and finely chopped
115 g (4 oz) carrots, peeled and thinly sliced
225 g (8 oz) brown-cap mushrooms, wiped and thinly sliced
115 ml (4 fl oz) dry white wine
335 g (12 oz) crème fraîche
4 × 15 ml tbs chopped fresh herbs, such as parsley, thyme and sage
115 g (4 oz) frozen petits pois
500 g dried pasta quills
extra mascarpone cheese, to serve (optional)

1. Blanch the asparagus or beans and leeks in boiling salted water for 3-4 minutes. Drain and rinse under cold running water.
2. Mix together the goat's cheese and mascarpone cheese.
3. Heat the butter with the oil in a large frying pan and fry the onion for 3 minutes, stirring,

Spring Vegetable Pasta

until softened. Add the carrots and mushrooms and continue to fry for 2-3 minutes, stirring occasionally, or until beginning to soften.
4. Add the remaining ingredients, except the cheese mixture, pasta and extra mascarpone, and simmer very gently until thickened.
5. Meanwhile, cook the pasta in boiling salted water for just 10-12 minutes, or until tender.

6. Remove the sauce from the heat and gently stir in the goat's cheese and mascarpone cheese mixture. Season to taste with salt and pepper.
7. Drain the pasta thoroughly and transfer to a warmed serving dish. Spoon on the hot sauce and serve immediately, topped with a spoonful of mascarpone, if wished.

31

PASTA WITH COURGETTES AND BROAD BEANS

SERVES 2

175 g (6 oz) dried tagliatelle or spaghetti
salt and freshly ground black pepper
175 g (6 oz) courgettes, thinly sliced
175 g (6 oz) frozen broad beans
150 g (5 oz) full-fat soft cheese with garlic
  and herbs
4 × 15 ml tbs milk or single cream
25 g (1 oz) walnut pieces, toasted

1. Cook the pasta in boiling salted water for 3 minutes. Add the courgettes and beans and cook for a further 7 minutes, or until the pasta is tender and the beans are cooked. Drain well.
2. Return the pasta and vegetables to the pan and heat gently while stirring in the cheese and milk; add more milk if necessary. Season.
3. Serve immediately, topped with the nuts.

PASTA WITH COURGETTE AND CARROT RIBBONS

SERVES 3-4

175 g (6 oz) courgettes
175 g (6 oz) carrots, peeled
225 g (8 oz) home-made broad ribbon pasta
  (see page 10)
salt and freshly ground black pepper
40 g (1½ oz) butter
½ × 5 ml tsp chopped fresh thyme

1. Using a swivel peeler, carefully pare the courgettes and peeled carrots into ribbons.
2. Cook the pasta in boiling salted water for about 10 minutes, adding the vegetable ribbons 1 minute before the end of cooking time. Drain and toss with the butter and thyme. Season and serve immediately.

Pasta with Courgette and Carrot Ribbons

Pasta with Watercress and Goat's Cheese

SERVES 4

335 g (12 oz) dried pasta shapes, such as spirals,
   bows and shells
salt and freshly ground black pepper
25 g (1 oz) fresh soft goat's cheese
3 × 15 ml tbs single cream
3 × 15 ml tbs roughly chopped watercress

1. Cook the pasta in boiling salted water for
10-12 minutes, or until just tender.
2. Beat together the cheese and cream.
3. Drain the pasta. Toss in the watercress and
cheese mixture. Season and serve immediately.

COOK'S TIP The heat of the freshly cooked
pasta wilts the watercress and melts the goat's
cheese mixture to form a sauce.

Spaghetti with Blue Cheese Sauce

SERVES 4

335 g (12 oz) dried spaghetti
salt and freshly ground black pepper
300 ml (10 fl oz) single cream
115 g (4 oz) Danish Blue cheese, roughly chopped

1. Cook the spaghetti in boiling salted water
for 10-12 minutes, or until just tender.
2. Heat the cream in a saucepan over a very
low heat and add the cheese.
3. Heat until the cheese has melted and season.
Drain the pasta and place in a warmed dish.
Pour the sauce over the pasta and serve.

Fresh Tagliatelle with Fennel

SERVES 6

1 large fennel bulb, trimmed and chopped
salt and freshly ground black pepper
75 g (3 oz) butter
2 large garlic cloves, skinned and crushed
1 × 5 ml tsp grated lemon rind
300 ml (10 fl oz) double cream
3 × 15 ml tbs chopped fresh fennel leaves
pinch of freshly grated nutmeg
juice of 1 lemon
335 g (12 oz) fresh plain tagliatelle or
   other noodles
335 g (12 oz) fresh spinach tagliatelle
75 g (3 oz) Parmesan cheese, grated

1. Blanch the fennel in a saucepan of boiling
salted water for 2 minutes. Drain well.
2. Melt half the butter in a pan and gently fry
the garlic for 2-3 minutes, stirring. Add the
blanched fennel and lemon rind and cook
gently for 3 minutes.
3. Add the remaining butter and the cream and
bring the mixture almost to the boil. Stir in the
fennel leaves, and add salt, pepper, nutmeg and
lemon juice to taste.
4. Meanwhile, cook the tagliatelle in boiling
salted water for 3-5 minutes, or until just
tender. Drain well.
5. Spoon half the fennel sauce over the pasta.
Add 25 g (1 oz) of the Parmesan cheese, and
toss until the sauce coats the pasta. Serve with
the remaining sauce and Parmesan cheese
handed separately.

COOK'S TIP The subtle aniseed flavour of
the fresh fennel goes perfectly with pasta in a
creamy sauce flavoured with garlic and lemon.

Pasta with Pecan and Parsley Sauce

SERVES 3

50 g (2 oz) pecan nuts shelled
25 g (1 oz) parsley sprigs
3 × 15 ml tbs freshly grated Parmesan cheese
115 ml (4 fl oz) olive oil
4 × 15 ml tbs curd or low-fat soft cheese
salt and freshly ground black pepper
335 g (12 oz) dried tricolour pasta twists
extra Parmesan cheese, to serve

1. Place the nuts and parsley in a blender or processor and blend until finely chopped.
2. Blend in the Parmesan cheese, then add the oil a little at a time, as if making mayonnaise. Stir in the curd cheese and seasoning.
3. Cook the pasta in boiling salted water for 10-12 minutes, or until just tender. Drain well and return to the rinsed-out saucepan.
4. Heat the sauce gently, without boiling. Stir into the pasta and serve with extra Parmesan.

Pasta with Leeks and Fromage Frais

SERVES 2

3 × 15 ml tbs olive oil
225 g (8 oz) leeks, trimmed, sliced and washed
150 ml (5 fl oz) vegetable stock
225-275 g (8-10 oz) dried pasta
salt and freshly ground black pepper
300 ml (10 fl oz) fromage frais
1 × 15 ml tbs horseradish relish
chopped fresh parsley, to garnish

1. Heat the oil in a saucepan and cook the leeks over a low heat for 4-5 minutes, or until the leeks begin to soften. Add the stock and bring

to the boil. Simmer, covered, for 15-20 minutes, or until the leeks are very soft.
2. Meanwhile, cook the pasta in boiling salted water for 10-12 minutes, or until just tender.
3. Stir the fromage frais and horseradish into the leek mixture. Season and heat gently, without boiling, stirring all the time.
4. Drain the pasta and transfer to a warmed serving bowl. Pour the sauce, over the pasta and serve, sprinkled with parsley.

Noodles in Walnut Sauce

SERVES 4

115 g (4 oz) walnut pieces
75 g (3 oz) butter, softened
1 small garlic clove, skinned and roughly chopped
2 × 15 ml tbs flour
300 ml (10 fl oz) milk
275 g (10 oz) fresh spinach tagliatelle
salt and freshly ground black pepper
115 g (4 oz) Cheddar cheese, grated
pinch of freshly grated nutmeg

1. In a blender or food processor, mix together the walnuts, 50 g (2 oz) of the butter and the garlic. Place in a bowl. Put the remaining of butter in the blender or food processor. Add the flour and milk. Work until evenly mixed.
2. Place the mixture in a saucepan and bring slowly to the boil, stirring. Simmer for 6 minutes. Meanwhile, cook the tagliatelle in boiling salted water until just tender. Drain thoroughly, then return to the pan. Add the nut butter and heat through gently, stirring.
3. Divide the pasta mixture between four large, individual gratin-type dishes. Add seasoning to the white sauce, then use to coat the pasta.
4. Scatter the grated cheese on top, sprinkle with the nutmeg, then grill for 5-10 minutes until brown and bubbling. Serve immediately.

Pasta with Leeks and Fromage Frais

NOODLES AND COURGETTES

SERVES 3

2 ripe tomatoes, skinned and chopped
1 × 15 ml tbs chopped fresh coriander
2 × 15 ml tbs chopped fresh parsley
grated rind and juice of 1 lemon
2 × 15 ml tbs olive oil
1 garlic clove, skinned and crushed
salt and freshly ground black pepper
115 g (4 oz) green beans, topped, tailed and halved
175 g (6 oz) courgettes, sliced
335 g (12 oz) fresh pasta
sprig of coriander, to garnish

1. Mix the tomatoes with the coriander, parsley, lemon rind and juice, oil, garlic and seasoning.
2. Steam the beans and courgettes for 5 minutes or until they are just tender. Drain.
3. Cook the pasta in boiling salted water for 3-5 minutes, or until just tender. Drain.
4. Place the tomato mixture in the pan and heat through gently. Add the steamed vegetables and mix them together lightly. Serve immediately with the pasta.

NEAPOLITAN TORTELLONI

SERVES 4

2 × 5 ml tsp sunflower oil
2 garlic cloves, skinned and finely chopped
225 ml (8 fl oz) passata or other sieved tomatoes
½ × 5 ml tsp dried oregano
salt and freshly ground black pepper
2 × 250 g packets fresh spinach tortelloni
15 g (½ oz) Parmesan cheese, freshly grated

1. Heat the oil in a large non-stick saucepan and gently cook the garlic until beginning to change colour. Add the passata and oregano. Season. Bring to the boil, turn off the heat and cover. Keep warm while cooking the pasta.

2. Cook the tortelloni in boiling salted water according to packet instructions, or until just tender. Drain well.
3. Divide the tortelloni between four soup plates, pour the sauce over and sprinkle with the Parmesan cheese.

TORTELLINI AL FORNO

SERVES 4

450 g (1 lb) aubergines, washed and trimmed
salt and freshly ground black pepper
25 g (1 oz) butter or margarine
450 g (1 lb) tomatoes, skinned and chopped
1 garlic clove, skinned and crushed
225 g (8 oz) tortellini
150 ml (5 fl oz) milk
225 g (8 oz) full-fat soft cheese
1 × 15 ml tbs grated Parmesan cheese
2 × 15 ml tbs dried breadcrumbs

1. Chop the aubergines, sprinkle with salt and leave for 15-20 minutes. Rinse well and pat dry.
2. Melt the butter in a frying pan, add the aubergines, tomatoes and garlic and cook gently for 5-10 minutes, until very soft. Season well.
3. Cook the tortellini in boiling salted water for 10-12 minutes for dried pasta, 5-8 minutes for fresh pasta, or until just tender. Drain well.
4. Spoon the vegetable mixture into a shallow ovenproof dish. Layer the tortellini on top.
5. In a bowl, gradually beat the milk into the cheese, whisking until smooth. Stir in 1 × 5 ml tsp Parmesan cheese. Spoon evenly over the tortellini. Sprinkle the top with breadcrumbs and the remaining Parmesan.
6. Bake in the oven at 200°C/400°F/Gas Mark 6 for 25-30 minutes until the top is golden. Serve immediately.

Noodles and Courgettes

Spinach and Ricotta Cannelloni

SERVES 4–6

4 × 15 ml tbs olive oil
2 small onions, skinned and finely chopped
2 × 15 ml tbs tomato purée
1 × 5 tsp mild paprika
2 × 400 g cans chopped tomatoes
pinch of dried oregano
300 ml (10 fl oz) dry red wine or vegetable stock
large pinch of sugar
salt and freshly ground black pepper
1 garlic clove, skinned and crushed
450 g (1 lb) frozen leaf spinach, thawed
   and drained
450 g (1 lb) ricotta cheese
pinch of freshly grated nutmeg
18 small sheets of lasagne, cooked
freshly grated Parmesan cheese
chopped fresh parsley, to garnish

1. Heat half the oil in a heavy-based saucepan, and fry half the onion for 5-10 minutes until very soft. Add the tomato purée and paprika and fry for 2-3 minutes.
2. Add the tomatoes, oregano, red wine and sugar, and season with salt and pepper. Simmer for 20 minutes, stirring occasionally.
3. Heat the remaining oil in a large saucepan and fry the garlic and remaining onion for 5 minutes, stirring all the time. Add the spinach and cook for 2 minutes. Cool slightly. Stir in the ricotta. Season with nutmeg, salt and pepper.
4. Lay the lasagne sheets on a work surface and divide the spinach mixture between them. Roll up the sheets to enclose the filling.
5. Arrange, seam-side down in a single layer, in a greased ovenproof serving dish. Pour the sauce over and sprinkle with Parmesan cheese. Bake in the oven at 200°C/400°F/Gas Mark 6 for 30 minutes. Serve immediately, garnished with chopped parsley.

Egg and Artichoke with Fresh Noodles

SERVES 4

450 g (1 lb) Jerusalem artichokes, peeled and cut
   into large chunks
142 ml pot soured cream
salt and freshly ground black pepper
2 × 250 g packets fresh tagliatelle, or other
   noodles
6 eggs, hard-boiled, shelled and quartered

1. Put the artichokes into a medium saucepan and cover with water. Bring to the boil, then simmer for 15-20 minutes or until they are very tender.
2. Drain the artichokes well. Purée in a blender or food processor until smooth.
3. Add the soured cream to the artichoke purée and season to taste.
4. Cook the pasta in boiling salted water for 3-5 minutes, or until just tender.
5. Drain well. Cover the base of four shallow, lightly greased flameproof dishes with the noodles.
6. Arrange the eggs over the noodles. Spoon the artichoke sauce evenly over each dish.
7. Place under a hot grill for 3-4 minutes until golden. Serve immediately.

COOK'S TIP Jerusalem artichokes have a pleasant and distinctive flavour and texture. The small, brown, knobbly tubers are tricky to peel, so bear this in mind when shopping and do not choose any that are too small or lumpy.

Spinach and Ricotta Cannelloni

CAULIFLOWER, LEEK AND MACARONI CHEESE

SERVES 4

1 cauliflower, about 900 g (2 lb), divided
   into florets
salt and freshly ground black pepper
75 g (3 oz) macaroni
225 g (8 oz) leeks, thickly sliced
50 g (2 oz) butter or margarine
1 × 15 ml tbs chopped fresh thyme
50 g (2 oz) plain flour
750 ml (1¼ pt) milk
150 g (5 oz) Cheddar cheese, grated
2 × 15 ml tbs grated Parmesan cheese
4 × 15 ml tbs fresh brown breadcrumbs
4 × 15 ml tbs coarse or medium oatmeal

1. Place the cauliflower florets in a saucepan of boiling salted water with the macaroni. Boil for 5 minutes. Add the leeks and boil for about another 5 minutes or until all are just tender. Drain well.
2. Melt the butter in a medium saucepan. Stir in the thyme, flour and milk. Bring to the boil, whisking continuously until slightly thickened. Off the heat, stir in half of the grated Cheddar cheese and half of the Parmesan. Season.
3. Stir the vegetable and macaroni mixture into the sauce. Spoon into a large, shallow ovenproof dish. Sprinkle over the breadcrumbs, oatmeal and remaining grated cheese.
4. Bake at 180°C/350°F/Gas Mark 4 for about 35 minutes or until piping hot. Brown under a hot grill if necessary.

VARIATION Substitute 4 × 5 ml tsp English mustard powder for the chopped thyme to give the sauce a slightly tangy flavour.

MACARONI CHEESE WITH BROCCOLI

SERVES 2

75 g (3 oz) macaroni
salt and freshly ground black pepper
25 g (1 oz) butter or margarine
25 g (1 oz) plain flour
300 ml (10 fl oz) milk
75 g (3 oz) Red Leicester cheese, grated
115 g (4 oz) broccoli florets
1 × 15 ml tbs fresh wholemeal breadcrumbs

1. Cook the pasta in boiling salted water for 15 minutes, or until just tender. Drain well.
2. Put the butter, flour and milk in a saucepan. Heat, whisking continuously, until the sauce boils, thickens and is smooth. Simmer for 1-2 minutes.
3. Remove the pan from the heat, add most of the cheese and stir until melted. Season to taste.
4. Blanch the broccoli in boiling water for 7 minutes, or until tender. Drain well.
5. Put the broccoli in the base of a 900 ml (1½ pt) flameproof serving dish. Cover with the macaroni and cheese sauce. Sprinkle with the remaining cheese and breadcrumbs. Brown under a hot grill.

COOK'S TIP Macaroni cheese has been popular family fare since Victorian times, when it was fashionable to give a British slant to traditional Italian dishes. This modern version uses British Red Leicester cheese and broccoli.

Macaroni Cheese with Broccoli

VEGETABLE LASAGNE

SERVES 6

2 × 15 ml tbs olive oil
I garlic clove, skinned and crushed
I carrot, trimmed, peeled and chopped
I large onion, skinned and sliced
I red pepper, cored, seeded and chopped
I × 15 ml tbs mild paprika
2 × 5 ml tsp dried oregano or marjoram
I large aubergine, trimmed and cut into chunks
225 g (8 oz) button mushrooms, wiped and sliced
2 large courgettes, trimmed and sliced
2 × 400 g cans chopped tomatoes
2 × 15 ml tbs tomato purée
2 bay leaves
225 g (8 oz) dried lasagne
Parmesan or Cheddar cheese, grated (optional)
BÉCHAMEL SAUCE:
900 ml (1½ pt) milk
I bay leaf
75 g (3 oz) butter
75 g (3 oz) plain flour
pinch of freshly grated nutmeg
salt and freshly ground black pepper

1. Heat the oil in a large saucepan. Add the next 4 ingredients and fry for 1-2 minutes or until beginning to soften. Add the paprika, herbs and aubergine and fry for a few minutes.
2. Add the remaining vegetables to the pan with the tomatoes, tomato purée and bay leaves. Bring to the boil, then reduce the heat, cover and simmer for 30 minutes. Remove the bay leaves.
3. Make the sauce. Put the milk and bay leaf in a saucepan and slowly bring to the boil. Remove from the heat. Melt the butter in a separate saucepan. Add the flour and cook over a low heat for 1-2 minutes, stirring with a wooden spoon. Discard the bay leaf and blend in the milk. Bring to the boil and cook, stirring, until the sauce thickens. Simmer for 2-3 minutes. Add the nutmeg and season.

4. Meanwhile, if using dried lasagne that needs pre-cooking, cook it in boiling salted water according to the packet instructions. Drain and leave to dry on a clean tea towel.
5. Spread a small amount of the tomato sauce in the base of a 3 lt (5 pt) ovenproof dish. Cover with a layer of lasagne and top with a layer of béchamel sauce. Continue in this way, ending with a layer of sauce. Sprinkle with cheese, if using.
6. Bake at 200°C/400°F/Gas Mark 6 for 45-60 minutes or until piping hot and browned. Leave to stand for 15 minutes before serving.

PASTA AND PEPPER GRATIN

SERVES 4

335 g (12 oz) dried pasta shells
salt and freshly ground black pepper
175 g (6 oz) low-fat soft cheese
175 g (6 oz) houmous
grated rind and juice I lemon
150 ml (5 fl oz) single cream
I × 15 ml tbs olive oil
I green pepper, seeded and cut into thin strips
I red pepper, seeded and cut into thin strips
3 × 15 ml tbs chopped fresh parsley
5 × 15 ml tbs freshly grated Parmesan cheese

1. Cook the pasta shells in boiling salted water for 10-12 minutes, or until just tender. Drain.
2. Mix together the low-fat soft cheese, houmous, grated rind and lemon juice, cream and a little black pepper.
3. Heat the oil in a large frying pan and fry the peppers for 5 minutes, or until beginning to soften. Remove from the heat and stir in the pasta, the cheese mixture and parsley.
4. Spoon into a shallow gratin dish and sprinkle with Parmesan. Grill under a moderate heat until lightly browned. Serve immediately.

Vegetable Lasagne

FRESH TAGLIATELLE WITH SEAFOOD SAUCE

SERVES 6

2 × 15 ml tbs grapeseed oil

1 small onion, or 2 shallots, skinned and finely
  chopped

1 garlic clove, skinned and crushed

2 × 225 g packets ready-cooked seafood cocktail

470 g jar traditional-style pasta sauce

lemon juice, to taste

dry vermouth, to taste

salt and freshly ground black pepper

2 × 250 g packets fresh spinach tagliatelle or
  other noodles

fresh parsley, to garnish

1. Heat the oil in a large frying pan and fry the
onion and garlic for 3-5 minutes until just
beginning to colour.

2. Add the mixed seafood and sauce with a
little lemon juice and vermouth to taste. Add
the seasoning and heat gently.

3. Cook the pasta in boiling salted water for
3-5 minutes, or until just tender. Drain in a
colander, then add a splash of oil and some
pepper. Toss and serve with the sauce,
garnished with parsley.

COOK'S TIP Use dried spinach tagliatelle,
if preferred, and increase the cooking time to
10-12 minutes, or until the pasta is just tender.

Fresh Tagliatelle with Seafood Sauce

SUMMER PASTA

SERVES 2–3

175 g (6 oz) dried tagliatelle, spinach and plain
　　mixed, or other noodles
salt and freshly ground black pepper
2 good-sized tomatoes, skinned,
　　seeded and chopped
3-4 anchovy fillets, well drained and
　　finely chopped
6 × 15 ml tbs single cream
115 g (4 oz) peeled cooked prawns
198 g can mussels in vinegar, drained and rinsed
1 × 5 ml tsp tomato purée
1 garlic clove, skinned and crushed
freshly grated Parmesan cheese, to serve
extra whole prawns in shells and herb sprigs, to
　　garnish (optional)

1. Cook the pasta in boiling salted water for
10–12 minutes, or until just tender.
2. Meanwhile, place the chopped tomatoes and
anchovies in a saucepan with the single cream,
prawns, mussels, tomato purée, garlic and
seasoning and heat gently, stirring.
3. Drain the pasta well and stir into the sauce.
Serve immediately, garnished with whole
prawns in their shells and fresh herbs, if wished,
and with Parmesan cheese handed separately.

CREAMY TUNA AND PASTA

SERVES 4

225 g (8 oz) dried pasta, such as spirals or bows
salt and freshly ground black pepper
25 g (1 oz) butter
142 ml pot soured cream
1 × 5 ml tsp anchovy essence
2 × 15 ml tbs malt vinegar
200 g can tuna steaks in brine, drained and flaked
4 eggs, hard-boiled, shelled and finely chopped
4 × 15 ml tbs chopped fresh parsley

1. Cook the pasta in boiling salted water for
10–12 minutes, or until just tender. Drain well.
2. Melt the butter in a deep frying pan and toss
in the pasta. Stir in the soured cream, anchovy
essence and vinegar.
3. Add the tuna and eggs to the pan with the
parsley. Season well and warm through over a
low heat, stirring occasionally. Serve
immediately.

PASTA WITH MUSSEL AND TOMATO SAUCE

SERVES 4

225 g (8 oz) dried tagliatelle or other noodles
salt and freshly ground black pepper
40 g (1½ oz) butter or margarine
2 bunches of salad onions, sliced into 5 cm
　　(2 in) pieces
¼ × 5 ml tsp chilli powder
1 × 15 ml tbs plain flour
1 garlic clove, skinned and crushed
400 g can chopped tomatoes
50 ml (2 fl oz) dry white wine
1 × 5 ml tsp sugar
200 g can tuna steaks in brine, drained and flaked
225 g (8 oz) frozen cooked mussels, thawed
coarsely grated fresh Parmesan cheese, to serve

1. Cook the pasta in boiling salted water for
10–12 minutes, or until just tender. Drain well.
2. Meanwhile, melt the butter in a medium
saucepan and fry the onions for 3–5 minutes
until just beginning to colour. Stir in the chilli
powder, flour and garlic and cook, stirring, for
1–2 minutes.
3. Mix in the tomatoes, wine, sugar and
seasoning. Bring to the boil, then carefully stir
in the tuna and mussels. Heat through for a few
minutes. Adjust the seasoning.
4. To serve, spoon the sauce over the pasta and
top with coarsely grated Parmesan cheese.

Summer Pasta

CREAMY PASTA WITH PRAWNS

SERVES 4

225 g (8 oz) dried pasta shells or spirals
salt and freshly ground black pepper
1 × 15 ml tbs oil
75 g (3 oz) bunch of salad onions, sliced
1 garlic clove, skinned and crushed
1 × 5 ml tsp tomato purée
6 × 15 ml tbs fromage frais or single cream
115 g (4 oz) cooked peeled prawns
200 g can tuna steaks in brine, drained and flaked
small bunch of fresh basil
4 × 15 ml tbs water
salad onion shreds and basil, to garnish (optional)

1. Cook the pasta in boiling salted water for 10–12 minutes, or until just tender.
2. Heat the oil in a medium saucepan. Add the onions and crushed garlic and stir-fry for 1 minute. Stir in the tomato purée, fromage frais or single cream, prawns and tuna with a little chopped fresh basil and the water and simmer for 2-3 minutes to heat through.
3. Drain the pasta then return to the pan. Pour over the sauce, stirring to mix. Warm gently to heat through. Add seasoning and garnish with salad onion shreds and basil, if wished.

COOK'S TIP Serve with a crisp green salad, tossed in a light vinaigrette dressing.

47

PASTA WITH TUNA AND OLIVE SAUCE

SERVES 4

50 g (2 oz) can anchovy fillets
milk, for soaking
1 × 15 ml tbs olive oil
1 onion, skinned and chopped
1 garlic clove, skinned and crushed
1 × 5 ml tsp dried marjoram
400 g can chopped tomatoes
335 g (12 oz) dried pasta shapes
salt and freshly ground black pepper, to taste
200 g can tuna steaks in brine, well drained
   and flaked
50 g (2 oz) black or green olives
2 × 15 ml tbs dry white wine
fresh marjorm, to garnish (optional)
coarsely grated Parmesan cheese, to serve

1. To remove the salt from the anchovies, drain well and place in a bowl. Cover with milk and soak for 20 minutes. Drain, pat dry and chop.
2. To make the sauce, heat the oil in a saucepan and gently cook the onion for 5 minutes. Add the garlic, marjoram and tomatoes with their juices. Bring to the boil and simmer for 15 minutes, stirring occasionally, until slightly thickened.
3. Meanwhile, cook the pasta in boiling salted water for 10-12 minutes, or until just tender.
4. Add the tuna fish, anchovies and olives to the sauce. Return to the boil, stirring, then simmer for 2-3 minutes. Stir in the wine and pepper. Drain the pasta and serve hot with the sauce spooned over. Garnish with fresh marjoram, if wished, and top with coarsely grated Parmesan.

COOK'S TIP There is no need to add any salt to the sauce as the anchovies contain enough residual salt to season this dish.

FISH-STUFFED CANNELLONI WITH CHEESE

SERVES 4

50 g (2 oz) butter or margarine
115 g (4 oz) mushrooms, wiped and chopped
1 small red pepper, seeded and diced
1 garlic clove, skinned and crushed
200 g can salmon or tuna, drained and flaked
50 g (2 oz) fresh breadcrumbs
12 dried cannelloni
SAUCE:
50 g (2 oz) butter or margarine
4 × 15 ml tbs plain flour
600 ml (20 fl oz) milk
175 g (6 oz) Cheddar cheese, grated
salt and freshly ground black pepper

1. Melt the butter in a saucepan and fry the mushrooms and red pepper for 2-3 minutes, until soft. Add the garlic, fish and breadcrumbs. Cook over a low heat for 5 minutes, stirring.
2. To make the sauce, melt the butter in a saucepan. Stir in the flour and cook for 1 minute, stirring. Remove the pan from the heat and gradually stir in the milk. Bring to the boil, then simmer, stirring, until thickened.
3. Remove from the heat and stir in 150 g (5 oz) of the cheese until melted. Season well.
4. Spoon the fish filling into the cannelloni so that it protrudes slightly at each end.
5. Pour enough sauce into an ovenproof serving dish to just cover the bottom. Arrange the cannelloni side by side in the dish and pour the remaining sauce over them. Sprinkle the rest of the cheese over the top.
6. Bake in the oven at 200°C/400°F/Gas Mark 6 for 30 minutes until golden. Serve immediately.

Pasta with Tuna and Olive Sauce

MEATY PASTA DISHES

PORK AND PASTA SUPPER

SERVES 4

450 g (1 lb) supertrim pork, cut into thin strips
75 g (3 oz) streaky bacon, rinded and finely
   chopped
225 g (8 oz) onions, preferably red, skinned and
   finely sliced
1 × 15 ml tbs wholegrain mustard
115 ml (4 fl oz) dry cider
1 garlic clove, skinned and crushed
3 × 15 ml tbs vegetable oil
salt and freshly ground black pepper
175 g (6 oz) green beans, topped, tailed and halved
1 red pepper, seeded and cut into strips
75 g (3 oz) dried pasta shapes
1 × 15 ml tbs soy sauce
4 × 15 ml tbs chicken stock

1. Place the pork, bacon and onions together in
a bowl and stir in the mustard, cider, garlic,
1 × 15 ml tbs of the oil and seasoning. Stir to
mix. Cover and refrigerate overnight. Allow at
least 8 hours marinating time for the flavours to
develop.
2. The next day, blanch the green beans and
red pepper in boiling salted water for 2
minutes. Drain well, then run under cold water
and set aside to cool.
3. Cook the pasta in boiling salted water for
10-12 minutes, or until just tender. Drain well.
4. Meanwhile, drain the meat from the
marinade, reserving the juices. Heat the
remaining oil in a large frying pan and stir-fry
the meat and onions over a high heat for 3-4
minutes until lightly browned.
5. Stir in the beans, pepper and pasta with the
marinade, soy sauce, stock and seasoning. Bring
to the boil, then simmer for about 5 minutes,
stirring occasionally, until piping hot. Adjust
the seasoning and serve immediately.

Pork and Pasta Supper

30-Minute Pork in Mustard

SERVES 4

175 g (6 oz) dried pasta shapes, such as shells,
  bows or spirals
salt and freshly ground black pepper
4 × 15 ml tbs olive oil
2 garlic cloves, skinned and crushed
450 g (1 lb) supertrim pork, very thinly sliced
50 g (2 oz) butter
225 g (8 oz) button mushrooms, wiped
  and sliced
2 × 15 ml tbs wholegrain mustard
4 × 15 ml tbs chopped fresh chives

1. Cook the pasta in boiling salted water for 10-12 minutes, or until just tender.
2. Drain the pasta well and return to the rinsed-out saucepan. Toss with 1 × 15 ml tbs of the olive oil.
3. Heat the remaining oil in a large frying pan, preferably non-stick, with the garlic. Add the pork, a little at a time, and brown well over a high heat for 2-3 minutes, stirring. Remove with a slotted spoon. Continue until all the meat is browned.
4. Add the butter, mushrooms and mustard and cook, stirring, for about 2 minutes. Return the pork to the pan with the pasta and continue to stir together over a high heat until the mixture is piping hot.
5. Add the seasoning and serve immediately, garnished with chopped fresh chives.

Broccoli and Ham Tagliatelle

SERVES 4

450 g (1 lb) dried spinach or plain tagliatelle, or
  other noodles
salt and freshly ground black pepper
50 g (2 oz) butter or margarine
115 g (4 oz) onion, skinned and sliced
225 g (8 oz) small broccoli florets
115 g (4 oz) yellow pepper, seeded and chopped
25 g (1 oz) plain flour
600 ml (20 fl oz) milk
225 g (8 oz) cooked ham, chopped
½ × 5 ml tsp freshly grated nutmeg
115 g (4 oz) Cheddar cheese, grated

1. Cook the pasta in boiling salted water for 10-12 minutes, or until tender. Drain well and keep warm in the rinsed-out pan.
2. Meanwhile, melt the butter in a large saucepan and lightly fry the onion, broccoli and yellow pepper for 3-5 minutes until beginning to soften.
3. Stir in the flour and cook for 1 minute, stirring. Remove the pan from the heat and add the milk, ham, nutmeg and seasoning. Return to the heat and bring to the boil, stirring. Cook for 1-2 minutes, then adjust the seasoning.
4. Stir the sauce and cooked pasta together and place in a shallow, flameproof dish. Scatter with the Cheddar cheese and grill until golden. Serve immediately.

VARIATION For a delicious vegetarian alternative, omit the ham and use any vegetables that can be cooked quickly, such as mangetout, mushrooms or leeks.

Fresh Tortellini with Cream

SERVES 6

50 g (2 oz) butter
275 g (10 oz) chicken breast, skinned,
    boned and chopped
115 g (4 oz) Parma ham, finely chopped
75 g (3 oz) Parmesan cheese, freshly grated
2 eggs, lightly beaten
pinch of freshly grated nutmeg
salt and freshly ground pepper
Home-Made Pasta Dough made with 3 eggs and
    300 g (11 oz) strong white flour (see page 10),
    plus extra flour for dusting
2 × 15 ml tbs vegetable oil
300 ml (10 fl oz) double cream

1. Melt 25 g (1 oz) butter in a large frying pan
and cook the chicken for about 5 minutes,
stirring, until cooked but tender. Remove from
the heat and leave to cool for 10 minutes.
2. Put the chicken in a blender or food
processor with the Parma ham, 50 g (2 oz) of
the Parmesan cheese, the eggs, nutmeg and salt
and pepper to taste. Work until finely minced.
3. Cut the dough into 2 pieces. Wrap 1 piece in
clingfilm. Roll out the other piece on a floured
surface to a 66 × 23 cm (26 × 9 in) rectangle.
4. Cut out rounds with a 5 cm (2 in) pastry
cutter, reserving the trimmings to make more
tortellini.
5. Working quickly to prevent the pasta drying
out, place ½ × 5 ml tsp filling on each round.
6. Brush the edges with water and fold in half,
the top edge and the bottom edge not quite
meeting. Press well together to seal.
7. Curl the two ends of the semicircle into a
ring around your index finger until the ends
touch. At the same time, turn the sealed edge of
the dough towards the fold to make a groove
around the edge. Seal the ends together firmly.
8. Spread the tortellini out in a single layer on a
floured tea towel while making the remainder.
Leave to dry for 30 minutes before cooking.

9. Place the oil and a few tortellini in a large
saucepan of lightly salted, boiling water to the
boil. Cook for 3–5 minutes, until just tender.
10. Remove with a slotted spoon and place in a
warmed buttered serving dish. Keep hot while
cooking the remainder of the tortellini.
11. In a separate saucepan, melt the rest of the
butter, add the cream, bring to the boil and
cook until slightly thickened. Stir in the rest of
the Parmesan cheese and mix well. Pour over
the tortellini and serve immediately.

Noodles with Hot Ham and Parmesan Cream

SERVES 4

450 g (1 lb) fresh pasta, cut into wide strips if
    home-made
salt and freshly ground black pepper
335 g (12 oz) fresh asparagus or French beans,
    trimmed and cut into 8 cm (3 in) lengths
115 g (4 oz) leeks, trimmed, finely shredded
    and washed
150 ml (5 fl oz) single cream
50 g (2 oz) Parmesan cheese, freshly grated
50 g (2 oz) Parma ham, or thinly sliced cooked
    ham, chopped

1. Cook the pasta in boiling salted water for
5–6 minutes, or until just tender. Drain well.
2. Meanwhile, cook the asparagus or beans in
boiling salted water for 7–10 minutes, or until
just tender. Add the leeks and boil for 30
seconds, then drain well.
3. Place the cream in a small saucepan with half
the cheese. Heat until just boiling, stirring.
4. Toss together the hot vegetables, pasta, ham
and remaining cheese. Season. Hand the
Parmesan cream around separately. Serve
immediately.

Noodles with Hot Ham and Parmesan Cream

PASTA WITH PEPERAMI AND MUSHROOMS

SERVES 3–4

175 g (6 oz) dried pasta shapes, such as shells
   or quills
salt and freshly ground black pepper
142 ml pot carton soured cream
3 × 15 ml tbs double cream
40 g (1½ oz) butter
175 g (6 oz) onions, skinned and thinly sliced
½ red pepper, seeded and finely shredded
115 g (4 oz) button mushrooms, wiped and
   quartered
2 × 25 g peperami sticks, thinly sliced
1 garlic clove, skinned and crushed
chopped fresh parsley, to garnish

1. Cook the pasta in boiling salted water for
10-12 minutes, or until just tender. Drain well.
2. Whisk together the soured cream, double
cream and seasoning.
3. Melt the butter in a large frying pan and fry
the onions and red pepper. Cover and cook
over a moderate heat until beginning to soften.
4. Increase the heat and stir in the mushrooms,
peperami, pasta and garlic. Stir over a high heat
until all the ingredients are piping hot.
5. Remove from the heat and immediately stir
in the cream mixture. There should be
sufficient heat to warm the cream mixture. If
not, stir over a gentle heat for a further few
seconds to warm through.
6. Garnish with the chopped parsley and serve
immediately.

COOK'S TIP Serve this rich pasta dish in
small helpings with a green salad and hot
crusty bread.

TURKEY PAPRIKA WITH PASTA

SERVES 4

1 × 15 ml tbs olive oil
1 small onion, skinned and sliced
450 g (1 lb) boneless turkey breast, skinned and
   cut into strips
1 × 15 ml tbs paprika
450 ml (16 fl oz) chicken stock
salt and freshly ground black pepper
1 green pepper, seeded and sliced
115 g (4 oz) small wholemeal pasta shapes,
   such as spirals
2 × 15 ml tbs soured cream
fresh parsley and paprika, to garnish

1. Heat the oil in a large frying pan and fry the
onion for 5 minutes, or until golden.
2. Add the turkey and paprika to the pan and
stir over a moderate heat for 2 minutes.
3. Stir in the stock and seasoning and bring to
the boil. Add the green pepper and pasta, cover
and simmer gently for 15-20 minutes until the
turkey and pasta are tender.
4. Stir in the soured cream and adjust the
seasoning. Garnish with freshly parsley and a
little paprika, then serve immediately.

COOK'S TIP Paprika is a red pepper prepared
from dried sweet peppers from Spain and
Hungary. The flavour can vary from mild to
hot. The best quality paprika is mild, sweet and
bright red.

Turkey Paprika with Pasta

Italian-Style Meatballs

SERVES 4

2 × 15 ml tbs olive oil
I large onion, skinned and finely chopped
2 garlic cloves, skinned and crushed
400 g can chopped tomatoes
2 × 5 ml tsp dried mixed herbs
2 × 5 ml tsp dried oregano
salt and freshly ground black pepper
450g (I lb) minced beef
50 g (2 oz) fresh white breadcrumbs
50 g (2 oz) Parmesan cheese, freshly grated
I egg, beaten
20 small stoned black olives
vegetable oil, for deep-frying
115 ml (4 fl oz) red or white dry
   Italian wine
300 ml (10 fl oz) water
225 g (8 oz) dried tagliatelle or spaghetti

1. Heat the oil in a heavy-based saucepan, add the onion and half of the garlic. Fry gently for 5 minutes or until lightly coloured.
2. Add the tomatoes, half of the herbs and salt and pepper to taste. Bring to the boil, stirring, then lower the heat, cover and simmer for about 20 minutes.
3. Meanwhile, make the meatballs. Put the minced beef in a bowl with the breadcrumbs, Parmesan cheese, remaining garlic and herbs. Mix well with your hands, then add salt and pepper to taste and bind with the beaten egg.
4. Pick up a small amount of the mixture, about the size of a walnut. Press one olive in the centre, then shape the mixture around it. Repeat with the remaining olives and meat to make 20 meatballs altogether.
5. Heat the oil in a deep-fat fryer to 190°C/375°F. Deep-fry the meatballs in batches for 2-3 minutes until lightly browned, then drain thoroughly on kitchen paper.
6. Stir the wine into the tomato sauce, then add the water and meatballs. Shake the pan to coat the balls in the sauce, adding more water if necessary. Cover and simmer for 15 minutes.
7. Meanwhile, place the pasta in a large pan of boiling salted water and cook until just tender. Drain, then spoon the meatballs and sauce over the top, then serve.

Chilli Beef with Noodles

SERVES 4

2 × 15 ml tbs olive oil
450 g (I lb) rump steak, trimmed and cut into
   bite-sized pieces
225 g (8 oz) red pepper, seeded and cut into
   bite-sized pieces
225 g (8 oz) broccoli, stalks sliced and head cut
   into florets
115 g (4 oz) onion, skinned and chopped
½ × 5 ml tsp chilli powder, or a few drops of
   Tabasco sauce
2 × 5 ml tsp dried oregano or dried mixed herbs
50 g (2 oz) dried tagliarini or other noodles
2 × 15 ml tbs sherry or medium white wine
300 ml (10 fl oz) beef stock
I × 15 ml tbs soy sauce
freshly ground black pepper
fresh oregano, to garnish

1. Heat the oil in a large saucepan and brown the beef well on all sides for about 2-3 minutes. Remove with a slotted spoon.
2. Add the vegetables, chilli powder and oregano and cook, stirring, for 1-2 minutes.
3. Mix in the tagliarini, sherry, stock and soy sauce. Cover and simmer for 5 minutes, or until the noodles and broccoli are tender.
4. Return the beef to the pan. Bring to the boil, then simmer for 1 minute to heat through. Season with pepper and serve immediately, garnished with fresh oregano.

Chilli Beef with Noodles

Beef Patties with Spaghetti and Pesto

SERVES 4

6 × 15 ml tbs olive oil
115 g (4 oz) onion, chopped
450 g (1 lb) lean minced beef
3 × 15 ml tbs chopped parsley
salt and freshly ground black pepper
175 g (6 oz) spaghetti
225 g (8 oz) shallots or small onions
25 g (1 oz) butter
50 g (2 oz) stoned black olives
2 × 5 ml tsp pesto sauce
Mozzarella cheese and anchovy fillets, to garnish

1. Heat 2 × 15 ml tbs oil in a large heavy-based frying pan and fry the onion for 2-3 minutes, then mix with the minced beef, chopped parsley and seasoning.
2. Shape into 12 patties and fry in 2 × 15 ml tbs olive oil for 5 minutes on each side or until well browned. Keep warm.
3. Meanwhile, cook the spaghetti in boiling salted water for 10–12 minutes, or until just tender. Drain.
4. Peel and thinly slice the shallots. Heat the butter with 2 × 15 ml tbs oil in a frying pan. Add the shallots and cook gently, stirring occasionally, for about 10–15 minutes, or until they are very soft and golden.
5. Stir in the black olives and pesto sauce. Warm through and adjust seasoning.

Beef Patties with Spaghetti and Pesto

6. Just before serving, top each beef patty with a slice of Mozzarella and a cross of anchovy fillets, and brown under a hot grill for 1 minute. Toss the spaghetti with the shallot mixture and serve immediately with the patties.

COOK'S TIP For an authentic Italian flavour garnish the pasta with fresh basil.

CHICKEN LIVER BOLOGNESE

SERVES 4

2 × 15 ml tbs olive oil

115 g (4 oz) onion, skinned and chopped

115 g (4 oz) smoked streaky bacon, rinded and chopped

225 g (8 oz) chicken livers, trimmed and roughly chopped

450 g (1 lb) lean minced beef

400 g can chopped tomatoes

150 ml (5 fl oz) dry red wine

2 × 5 ml tsp dried oregano or dried mixed herbs

2 × 15 ml tbs tomato purée

salt and freshly ground black pepper

450 g (1 lb) dried spaghetti or tagliatelle or other noodles

1. Heat the oil in a medium saucepan and fry the onion, bacon, chicken livers and beef for 4-5 minutes, until the meat breaks up, stirring all the time.

2. Add the remaining ingredients, except the pasta, cover and simmer for 25-30 minutes.

3. Cook the pasta in boiling salted water for 10-12 minutes, or until just tender.

4. Drain the pasta well. Divide between four heated serving plates. Serve the chicken liver mixture with the pasta.

SPICED LIVER SAUTÉ

SERVES 4

2 × 15 ml tbs olive oil

450 g (1 lb) lamb's liver, trimmed and cut into thin strips

115 g (4 oz) onion, skinned and sliced

115 g (4 oz) button mushrooms, wiped and sliced

115 g (4 oz) fine green beans, topped and tailed

1 × 15 ml tbs plain flour

1-2 × 5 ml tsp paprika

450 g (1 lb) dried tagliatelle or other noodles

150 ml (5 fl oz) vegetable stock

Tabasco sauce

salt and freshly ground black pepper

150 ml (5 fl oz) single cream

1. Heat the oil in a large frying pan and fry the liver, stirring, until browned. Lift out with a slotted spoon and set aside, keeping warm.

2. Add the onion, mushrooms and beans to the pan with a little more oil if necessary, and cook, stirring, for about 5 minutes, or until beginning to soften. Mix in the flour and paprika and cook for a further 1 minute.

3. Cook the pasta in boiling salted water for 10-12 minutes, or until just tender.

4. Add the stock, liver, Tabasco to taste and seasoning to the vegetables. Simmer, covered, for 5-10 minutes, or until the liver is cooked and the vegetables are just tender.

5. Stir in the cream, adjust seasoning and bubble up quickly.

6. Drain the pasta well. Divide between four heated serving plates. Serve the spicy liver mixture with the pasta.

COOK'S TIP If fresh, fine green beans are not available, use frozen ones.

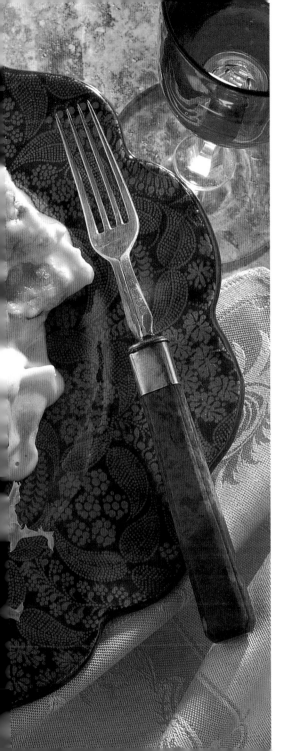

LAMB AU GRATIN

SERVES 8

65 g (2½ oz) butter
675 g (1½ lb) mushrooms, wiped and chopped
1 × 15 ml tbs vegetable oil
675 g (1½ lb) lean minced lamb
1 garlic clove, skinned and crushed
227 g can tomatoes, drained
75 g (3 oz) plain flour
2 × 15 ml tbs chopped fresh herbs
150 ml (5 fl oz) dry white wine
salt and pepper
16 sheets cooked lasagne
900 ml (1½ pt) milk
115 g (4 oz) Cheddar cheese, grated
115 g (4 oz) Mozzarella cheese, chopped

1. Melt 25 g (1 oz) of the butter in a large saucepan and cook the mushrooms over moderate heat for about 10 minutes until soft.
2. Heat the oil in a large frying pan and brown the lamb. Drain off all the fat.
3. Stir in the garlic, mushrooms, tomatoes, 2 × 15 ml tbs flour and the herbs. Cook for 1-2 minutes, then add the wine and seasoning. Bring to the boil, then simmer for about 30 minutes, uncovered. Cool for 10 minutes.
4. Spread the mixture over the sheets of lasagne and roll up each sheet from one short side.
5. Cut each roll into three pieces. Pack tightly together, standing upright, in a large, deep, straight-sided flameproof serving dish.
6. Melt the remaining butter in a saucepan. Add the remaining flour and cook over a low heat, stirring, for 2 minutes. Gradually blend in the milk. Bring to the boil slowly, then simmer for 2-3 minutes, stirring. Season.
8. Pour the sauce over the pasta and bake at 200°C/400°F/Gas Mark 6 for 40 minutes. Uncover, sprinkle with the cheeses and grill until golden. Serve immediately.

Lamb au Gratin

Beef and Veal Gratin

SERVES 4

2 × 15 ml tbs olive oil
225 g (8 oz) onions, skinned and finely chopped
115 g (4 oz) carrots, peeled and finely chopped
2 sticks celery, finely chopped
175 g (6 oz) red pepper, seeded and
   finely chopped
225 g (8 oz) each minced beef and minced veal
40 g (1½ oz) plus 1 × 5 ml tsp plain flour
300 ml (10 fl oz) beef stock
150 ml (5 fl oz) red wine
115 g (4 oz) Parma ham, finely chopped
2 × 15 ml tbs chopped fresh rosemary
1 bay leaf
salt and pepper
16 dried cannelloni
50 g (2 oz) butter
600 ml (20 fl oz) milk
50 g (2 oz) Parmesan cheese, grated

1. Heat the oil in a large frying pan and cook the onions, carrots, celery and pepper until the vegetables soften and begin to colour.
2. Add the beef and veal and cook over a high heat, stirring frequently, until the meat begins to brown. Stir in the 1 × 5 ml tsp flour and cook for a further minute.
3. Pour in the stock and red wine with the Parma ham, rosemary, bay leaf and the seasoning. Slowly bring to the boil, then cover and simmer gently for about 1 hour. (If necessary uncover the pan, increase the heat and cook until the mixture has reduced to a thick sauce.) Remove the bay leaf.
4. Cook the pasta in boiling salted water for 10-12 minutes, or until tender. Drain well.
5. Fill the cannelloni with the mince mixture and place in a single layer in a 2.4 lt (4 pt) ovenproof serving dish.
6. Melt the butter in a small saucepan. Add the remaining flour and cook, stirring, for 1-2 minutes before gradually adding the milk.

Bring to the boil, then simmer, stirring occasionally, for 2-3 minutes. Off the heat, beat in half the grated cheese and add the black pepper to taste. Spoon over the pasta and sprinkle with the remaining cheese.
7. Bake in the oven at 180°C/350°F/Gas Mark 4 for about 40 minutes, or until golden and bubbling. Serve immediately.

VARIATION If you wish, you can use beef only in this recipe by substituting an extra 225 g (8 oz) for the veal.

Macaroni Layer Pie

SERVES 4–6

1 × 15 ml tbs vegetable oil
450 g (1 lb) minced beef
115 g (4 oz) onion, skinned and chopped
1 garlic clove, skinned and crushed
400 g can chopped tomatoes
200 ml (7 fl oz) chicken or beef stock
1 × 5 ml tsp dried mixed herbs
salt and freshly ground black pepper
225 g (8 oz) dried macaroni
40 g (1½ oz) butter
3 × 15 ml tbs plain flour
450 ml (15 fl oz) milk
2 × 5 ml tsp Dijon mustard
115 g (4 oz) Cheddar cheese, grated

1. Heat the oil in a medium-sized saucepan and cook the mince and onion over a high heat for 5-8 minutes, or until they are lightly coloured. Break up the mince as you brown it, spreading it evenly around the pan, to prevent it forming into lumps.
2. Add the garlic, tomatoes with the juices, stock, herbs and seasoning. Bring to the boil and simmer, uncovered, for about 20 minutes, or until the mince is tender and the liquid well reduced. Adjust the seasoning.
3. Meanwhile, cook the macaroni in boiling

Macaroni Layer Pie

salted water for 10–12 minutes, or until just tender. Drain and rinse under cold running water, then drain for 2–3 minutes longer.

4. Layer the mince and pasta alternately in a lightly greased, large, deep ovenproof serving dish, ending with a pasta layer on the top.

5. Melt the butter in a saucepan. Add the flour and cook, stirring, for 1–2 minutes before gradually adding the milk. Bring to the boil,

then simmer for 2–3 minutes.

6. Off the heat, whisk in the mustard, half the grated Cheddar cheese and seasoning. Pour over the pasta and sprinkle with the remaining grated cheese.

7. Stand the dish on a baking tray and then bake in the oven at 200°C/400°F/Gas Mark 6 for 35–40 minutes, or until golden and thoroughly hot. Serve immediately.

PASTA PIE

SERVES 6

115 g (4 oz) butter
2 × 15 ml tbs olive oil
1 small onion, skinned and finely chopped
2 garlic cloves, skinned and crushed
400 g can tomatoes
1 × 5 ml tsp chopped fresh basil
salt and freshly ground pepper
225 g (8 oz) dried pasta, such as macaroni
75 g (3 oz) plain flour
600 ml (20 fl oz) milk
75 g (3 oz) Gruyère cheese, grated
4 × 15 ml tbs freshly grated Parmesan cheese
3 × 15 ml tbs dried breadcrumbs

1. Melt 50 g (2 oz) of the butter in a heavy-based saucepan with the oil. Gently fry the onion and garlic for 5 minutes until soft.
2. Add the tomatoes, basil and seasoning to taste, then stir with a wooden spoon to break up the tomatoes. Bring to the boil, then lower the heat and simmer for 10 minutes, stirring occasionally.
3. Meanwhile, cook the pasta in boiling salted water for 10 minutes, or until just tender; drain.
4. Melt the remaining butter in a separate saucepan, add the flour and cook over a low heat, stirring, for about 2 minutes. Remove from the heat and gradually blend in the milk, stirring after each addition to prevent lumps forming. Bring to the boil slowly, stirring, until the sauce thickens. Add the Gruyère cheese and seasoning to taste and stir until melted.
5. Mix the pasta with the tomato sauce. Arrange half of this mixture in a large, buttered ovenproof serving dish.
6. Pour over half of the cheese sauce. Repeat the layers, then sprinkle evenly with the Parmesan cheese and breadcrumbs.
7. Bake in the oven at 190°C/375°F/Gas Mark 5 for 15 minutes, then brown under a hot grill for 5 minutes. Serve immediately.

MACARONI BAKE

SERVES 4–6

175 g (6 oz) dried macaroni
salt and freshly ground black pepper
2 × 15 ml tbs olive oil
115 g (4 oz) onion, skinned and chopped
225 g (8 oz) button mushrooms, wiped and sliced
335 g (12 oz) tomatoes, skinned and chopped
300 ml (10 fl oz) vegetable stock
1 × 15 ml tbs tomato purée
1 × 5 ml tsp dried mixed herbs
1 × 5 ml tsp dried oregano
2 × 15 ml tbs plain wholemeal flour
300 ml (10 fl oz) milk
115 g (4 oz) low-fat soft cheese
1 egg, beaten
1 × 5 ml tsp English mustard powder
2 × 15 ml tbs wholemeal breadcrumbs
2 × 15 ml tbs grated Parmesan cheese

1. Cook the pasta in boiling salted water for 10-12 minutes or until just tender. Drain well.
2. Heat the oil in a separate pan and gently fry the onion for 5 minutes until soft.
3. Add the mushrooms to the pan, increase the heat and toss with the onion for 1-2 minutes.
4. Add the tomatoes and stock and bring to the boil, stirring constantly to break up the tomatoes. Lower the heat and stir in the tomato purée, herbs and salt and pepper to taste. Simmer gently for 10 minutes.
5. Put the flour and milk in a food processor and blend for 1 minute. Transfer to a heavy-based pan and simmer until thickened.
6. Remove from the heat and beat in the cheese, egg, mustard and salt and pepper.
7. Mix the macaroni with the mushrooms in the tomato sauce, then pour into an ovenproof serving dish. Pour over the cheese sauce. Sprinkle with breadcrumbs and Parmesan.
8. Bake in the oven at 190°C/375°F/Gas Mark 5 for 20 minutes until golden and bubbling. Serve immediately.

Pasta and Mushrooms Baked with Two Cheeses

SERVES 2–3

225 g (8 oz) dried tagliatelle or other noodles
salt and freshly ground black pepper
25 g (1 oz) butter
1 garlic clove, skinned and crushed
225 g (8 oz) mushrooms, wiped and thinly sliced
50 g (2 oz) Stilton cheese
4 × 15 ml tbs double cream
1 egg, lightly beaten
115 g (4 oz) Mozzarella cheese, grated

1. Cook the pasta in boiling salted water for 10–12 minutes, or until tender. Drain well.
2. Meanwhile, melt the butter in a large frying pan and cook the garlic and mushrooms, stirring frequently, until just softened.
3. Crumble in the Stilton cheese and cook for a couple of minutes, stirring continuously. Stir in the cream and season to taste.
4. Season the pasta with lots of pepper. Mix into the mushroom sauce. Stir in the egg and mix together thoroughly.
5. Place the mixture into a buttered ovenproof serving dish and sprinkle the Mozzarella on top. Cover with foil and bake in the oven at 180°C/350°F/Gas Mark 4 for 10 minutes, then remove the foil and bake at 220°C/425°F/Gas Mark 7 for a further 10–15 minutes until brown and crusty on top. Serve immediately.

Pasta and Mushrooms Baked with Two Cheeses

Seafood Lasagne

SERVES 6

450 g (1 lb) fresh haddock fillet, skinned
300 ml (10 fl oz) white wine
slices of carrot, onion and bay leaf for flavouring
salt and freshly ground black pepper
200 g (7 oz) dried spinach lasagne
150 g (5 oz) butter
450 g (1 lb) leeks, trimmed, thickly sliced and washed
1 garlic clove, skinned and crushed
90 g (3½ oz) plain flour
150 ml (5 fl oz) single cream
142 ml pot soured cream
1 × 15 ml tbs chopped fresh dill
225 g packet seafood cocktail
50 g (2 oz) Cheddar or Gruyère cheese, grated
2 × 15 ml tbs grated Parmesan cheese
fresh dill and lemon slices, to garnish

1. Cover the haddock fillet with water and half the wine. Add the flavouring ingredients, season and bring to the boil. Cover and simmer for 5 minutes, or until tender.
2. Lift the fish on to a plate and flake the flesh, discarding any bones. Strain the cooking juices and make up to 1 lt (1¾ pt) with water.
3. Cook the lasagne according to the packet instructions, stirring occasionally with a fork. Drain and immediately run cold water over the pasta. Spread on a clean tea towel and cover.
4. Melt 50 g (2 oz) of the butter in a medium saucepan and gently cook the leeks and garlic, covered, for about 10 minutes. Remove from the pan using a slotted spoon.
5. Melt the remaining butter. Add the flour and cook, stirring, for 1 minute. Off the heat, stir in the reserved 1 lt (1¾ pt) stock and remaining wine. Bring to the boil, stirring, and cook for 2 minutes. Off the heat, whisk in the cream, soured cream and dill. Season.

6. Spoon a little of the sauce into a 3 lt (5¼ pt) shallow ovenproof serving dish. Top with a layer of pasta, followed by the haddock, seafood cocktail and leeks, and a little more sauce. Continue layering, finishing with the sauce. Scatter over the grated cheeses.
7. Cook in the oven at 200°C/400°F/Gas Mark 6 for 45-50 minutes. Cool slightly before serving, garnished with dill and lemon.

VARIATIONS

Creamy Chicken Lasagne Ingredients as for Seafood Lasagne, replacing the haddock and seafood cocktail with 1.4 kg (3 lb) oven-ready chicken, and the dill with 4 × 15 ml tbs chopped fresh basil or 1 × 5 ml tsp dried. Cover the chicken with water, half the wine and the flavouring as in step 1. Bring to the boil, then cover and simmer for 1 hour, or until tender. Cut the chicken into bite-sized pieces, discarding skin and bone. Reduce the cooking juices to about 1 lt (1¾ pt). Strain and skim. Complete the lasagne as in steps 3-7, whisking 2 × 15 ml tbs Dijon mustard into the sauce in step 5.

Leek and Mushroom Lasagne Ingredients as for Seafood Lasagne, replacing the haddock and seafood cocktail with 450 g (1 lb) mixed mushrooms (brown cap, flat, oyster, etc) and the dill with 4 × 15 ml tbs chopped fresh basil or 1 × 5 ml tsp dried. Increase the leeks to 675 g (1½ lb) and Cheddar or Gruyère cheese to 225 g (8 oz). Omit steps 1-2. Continue as in steps 3-4, then sauté the sliced mushrooms in the remaining 75 g (3 oz) butter for 3-4 minutes. Remove from the pan using a slotted spoon. Make the sauce as in step 5, adding more butter, if necessary and using 700 ml (24 fl oz) vegetable stock and 300 ml (10 fl oz) white wine with the basil in place of dill. Whisk in 2 × 15 ml tbs Dijon mustard. Complete as in steps 6-7, layering the mushrooms and some of the Cheddar or Gruyère in place of the fish.

Seafood Lasagne

Mushroom Lasagne

SERVES 6

225 g (8 oz) frozen leaf spinach, thawed
225 g (8 oz) dried lasagne
salt and freshly ground black pepper
115 g (4 oz) butter or margarine
900 g (2 lb) mixed mushrooms, such as button,
    flat and brown cap (chestnut), wiped and
    quartered or sliced
2 × 15 ml tbs lemon juice
75 g (3 oz) plain flour
600 ml (20 fl oz) milk
600 ml (20 fl oz) vegetable stock
freshly grated nutmeg, to taste
2 garlic cloves, skinned and crushed
175 g (6 oz) Gruyère cheese, grated
50 g (2 oz) fresh white breadcrumbs

1. Drain the spinach and squeeze out any
excess liquid. Chop finely.
2. Cook the pasta in boiling salted water
according to the packet instructions, until
tender. Drain and rinse under cold running
water. Spread the pasta out on a clean tea towel
and cover with a damp tea towel until
required.
3. Melt half the butter in a large pan. Add the
mushrooms and lemon juice, and season with
salt and pepper. Cover and cook over a fairly
high heat for 4-6 minutes, or until the
mushrooms are tender. Remove from the pan
with a slotted spoon, then bubble the juices to
evaporate any excess moisture until there is
only fat left in the saucepan.
4. Melt the remaining butter in the same
saucepan. Carefully stir in the flour and cook
for 1-2 minutes before slowly blending in the
milk and stock. Gradually bring to the boil,
making sure that you keep stirring all the time,
and cook for 1-2 minutes or until boiling and
thickened. Mix in the nutmeg, garlic and
spinach. Taste and adjust the seasoning if
necessary.

5. Spoon a little of the sauce into the base of a
3 lt (5 pt) ovenproof dish. Top with a layer of
pasta followed by a layer of mushrooms. Spoon
over more of the sauce, then continue layering
the ingredients, finishing with the sauce.
Sprinkle over the Gruyère and breadcrumbs.
6. Stand the dish on a baking tray and cook at
200°C/400°F/Gas Mark 6 for 45-60 minutes.
Serve immediately.

Three-Cheese Lasagne

SERVES 8

400 g can tomatoes
1 small onion, skinned and chopped
1 celery stick, chopped
1 garlic clove, skinned and crushed
1 bay leaf
salt and freshly ground black pepper
450 g (1 lb) minced beef
1 egg, lightly beaten
50 g (2 oz) Parmesan cheese, grated
75 g (3 oz) plain flour
4 × 15 ml tbs olive or vegetable oil
75 g (3 oz) butter
750 ml (1¼ pt) milk
115 g (4 oz) mild cured ham, chopped
115 g (4 oz) Mozzarella cheese, grated
115 g (4 oz) Bel Paese cheese, cut into strips
150 ml (5 fl oz) single cream
400 g (14 oz) lasagne

1. Place the tomatoes, onion, celery, garlic and
bay leaf in a small pan. Bring to the boil and
simmer, uncovered, for 30 minutes, stirring
occasionally.
2. Discard the bay leaf and rub mixture
through a sieve or purée in a blender. Season.
3. Combine the beef, egg, half the Parmesan
and seasoning. Shape the mixture into 24
meatballs. Roll lightly in a little seasoned flour.
4. Heat the oil in a frying pan and cook the
meatballs for about 5 minutes until brown.

Remove with a slotted spoon and drain.

5. Melt the butter in a pan, add 65 g (2½ oz) flour and cook for 1 minute, stirring. Remove from the heat and gradually stir in the milk.

6. Bring to the boil and cook, stirring, until the sauce thickens. Stir in the ham, Mozzarella, Bel Paese, cream and seasoning.

7. Prepare the lasagne as directed on the packet.

8. In a large, greased, ovenproof serving dish, layer up the lasagne, meatballs, tomato and white sauces, finishing with a layer of lasagne topped with white sauce.

9. Sprinkle the remaining Parmesan cheese over the top. Bake in the oven at 200°C/400°F/Gas Mark 6 for 20-25 minutes until golden. Serve immediately.

Mushroom Lasagne

BABY VEGETABLE AND PASTA SALAD

SERVES 6

335 g (12 oz) dried pasta shapes, such as shells,
   bows and spirals
salt and freshly ground black pepper
675 g (1½ lb) mixed baby vegetables, such as
   courgettes, asparagus tips, sugar snap peas,
   patty pan squashes and leeks
4 × 15 ml tbs olive oil
3 × 15 ml tbs pesto sauce
115 g (4 oz) black olives, stoned
115 g (4 oz) cherry tomatoes
handful of mixed salad leaves
a few chopped fresh herbs

1. Cook the pasta in boiling salted water for
10–12 minutes, or until just tender. Drain.
2. Meanwhile, prepare the mixed baby
vegetables, leaving them whole wherever
possible. Any larger, slower cooking vegetables
should be halved or quartered. Steam the
prepared vegetables until just tender.
3. Whisk together the olive oil and pesto sauce.
4. Put the pasta in a large bowl with the pesto
mixture, the steamed vegetables and the olives
and tomatoes. Toss well together.
5. To serve, put the salad leaves in the bottom
of a large serving bowl and spoon the pasta
mixture over the top. Sprinkle with herbs and
serve immediately.

COOK'S TIP This salad is meant to be served
lukewarm rather than hot or cold. However, if
you would like to make it in advance and serve
it cold, cool the vegetables and pasta
completely and refrigerate until required. Let
them come to room temperature before
spooning them on top of the salad leaves.

Baby Vegetable and Pasta Salad

BROCCOLI AND PASTA SALAD

SERVES 4

175 g (6 oz) wholewheat pasta spirals
salt and freshly ground black pepper
275 g (10 oz) broccoli florets and chopped stems
1 × 15 ml tbs sesame seeds
4 × 5 ml tsp sunflower oil
1 orange, peeled, segmented and chopped, with
   any juice reserved

1. Put the pasta in a saucepan half filled with
boiling salted water. Bring back to the boil and
place the broccoli in a sieve over the pan.
Cover and cook for 8 minutes or until the pasta
and broccoli are tender. Drain and place in a
large dish or bowl.
2. Place the sesame seeds in an ungreased
heavy-based frying pan and cook over a low
heat for 2-3 minutes or until the seeds are just
beginning to jump. Crush the seeds in a pestle
and mortar, grind them in a coffee grinder or
use the end of a rolling pin and a strong bowl.
3. Mix the sesame seeds, oil, orange pieces and
any orange juice in a serving bowl. Add the
broccoli and pasta, season and toss gently.
Cover and chill before serving.

PASTA WITH FETA AND CAULIFLOWER SALAD

SERVES 4

½ medium cauliflower, broken into florets
handful of fresh mint
115 g (4 oz) wholewheat pasta twists or shells
salt and freshly ground black pepper
50 g (2 oz) feta cheese
DRESSING:
2 × 15 ml tbs lemon juice
2 × 5 ml tsp olive oil

1. Steam the cauliflower with a couple of sprigs
of mint for about 8 minutes or until tender.
Drain well and put into a bowl.
2. Cook the pasta in boiling salted water for
10-12 minutes, or until tender. Drain and add
to the cauliflower. Crumble the feta over the
cauliflower and pasta. Chop a few sprigs of
fresh mint and add to the salad.
3. For the dressing, mix together the lemon
juice, oil and a generous amount of pepper and
pour over the salad. Serve immediately.

PARTY PASTA

SERVES 6

SALAD:
225 g (8 oz) dried pasta shapes, such as quills,
   shells or spirals
salt and freshly ground black pepper
225 g (8 oz) thin asparagus spears, trimmed and
   cut into finger-length pieces
225 g (8 oz) courgettes, coarsely grated
115 g (4 oz) Gruyère cheese, grated
115 g (4 oz) feta cheese, diced
DRESSING:
150 ml (5 fl oz) olive oil
2 × 15 ml tbs white wine vinegar
½ × 5 ml tsp sugar
2 × 5 ml tbs Dijon mustard
2 × 15 ml tbs chopped fresh herbs

1. Cook the pasta in boiling salted water for
10-12 minutes, or until just tender. Drain and
rinse under cold running water.
2. Cook the asparagus in boiling salted water
for 5-7 minutes, or until just tender. Drain and
rinse as above.
3. Whisk together all the dressing ingredients
and season.
4. Toss together all the ingredients. Serve
immediately, or refrigerate, covered, for up to
1 day. Stir before serving.

Party Pasta

PASTA SALAD WITH AVOCADO

SERVES 4

115 g (4 oz) dried wholewheat pasta shapes, such
as bows or shells
salt and freshly ground black pepper
3 × 15 ml tbs olive oil
1 × 15 ml tbs lemon juice
3 × 15 ml tbs fresh chopped parsley
1 × 15 ml tbs Dijon mustard
225 g (8 oz) smoked back bacon rashers, rinded
225 g (8 oz) cherry tomatoes, halved
2 ripe avocados
1 bunch of watercress, to serve

1. Cook the pasta in boiling salted water for
10-12 minutes or until just tender. Drain well.
2. Meanwhile, whisk together the oil, lemon
juice, parsley, seasoning and mustard.
3. Pour the dressing over the cooked warm
pasta and set aside to cool. Grill the bacon until
crispy. Snip into pieces and add to the pasta
with the tomatoes.
4. Just before serving, peel and dice the
avocado flesh and stir gently into the salad.
Serve on a bed of watercress.

COOK'S TIP Stir the avocado into the pasta at
the last minute to prevent it breaking up.

75

Chicken and Ham Pasta Salad

SERVES 8

225 g (8 oz) dried pasta bows
salt and freshly ground black pepper
225 g (8 oz) mangetout, trimmed
400 g can stoned black olives
115 g (4 oz) smoked cooked ham
450 g (1 lb) cooked chicken breast fillet
150 ml (5 fl oz) natural yogurt
3 × 15 ml tbs French dressing

1. Cook the pasta in boiling salted water for 10-12 minutes, or until just tender, adding the mangetout for the last 2 minutes of cooking time. Drain and cool under cold running water.
2. Halve the olives. Slice the ham and chicken, discarding any fat or skin. Mix with the pasta and mangetout.
3. Mix the yogurt and dressing. Toss the salad in it to coat. Season and serve at once.

Mixed Pasta Salad

SERVES 4

450 g (1 lb) firm white fish fillet, skinned and cut into chunks
450 g (1 lb) fennel, halved and sliced
150 ml (5 fl oz) dry vermouth
5 × 15 ml tbs water
salt and freshly ground black pepper
175 g (6 oz) dried pasta shapes, red and green mixed, such as shells, bows and spirals
450 g (1 lb) tomatoes, skinned, seeded and chopped, with the juices reserved
3 × 15 ml tbs olive oil
3 × 15 ml tbs chopped fresh dill or fennel

1. Place the fish, fennel, vermouth and water in a frying pan. Season, bring slowly to the boil, cover and simmer for 5 minutes, or until the fish is tender and flakes easily.
2. Meanwhile, cook the pasta in boiling salted water for 10-12 minutes, or until just tender. Drain well.
3. Using a slotted spoon, lift the fish and fennel out of the cooking liquid. Place in a large bowl with the pasta and tomatoes.
4. Add the tomato juices to the fish liquid, then boil until 175 ml (6 fl oz) remains.
5. Stir in the oil and seasoning. Mix half into the pasta with the herbs. Cover and leave in a cool place for 1-2 hours.
6. Before serving, stir in the remaining dressing.

Pasta Salad with Chicken and Pesto

SERVES 4

175 g (6 oz) dried mixed tricolour twists and egg pasta spirals
salt and freshly ground black pepper
1 × 15 ml tbs olive oil
1 × 15 ml tbs pesto sauce
1 garlic clove, skinned and crushed
6 salad onions, trimmed and sliced
1 bulb of fennel, sliced
115 g (4 oz) roast chicken, cut into strips
75 g (3 oz) cooked cured ham, cut into strips
175 g (6 oz) cherry tomatoes, halved
8 stoned black olives, halved
2 × 15 ml tbs chopped fresh mixed herbs

1. Cook the pasta in boiling salted water for 10-12 minutes, or until just tender.
2. Meanwhile, gently heat the oil, pesto sauce and garlic in a small pan.
3. Drain the pasta, place in a mixing bowl, pour over the pesto mixture and toss. Cool.
4. Add the salad onions, fennel, chicken, ham, tomatoes and olives to the pasta. Season. Place in a serving bowl and sprinkle with herbs.

Smoked Mackerel and Pasta Salad

SERVES 4

225 g (8 oz) dried pasta shapes, such as shells
  or spirals
salt and freshly ground black pepper
3 medium courgettes, about 275 g (10 oz) total
  weight, sliced
2 oranges
3 × 15 ml tbs olive oil
335 g (12 oz) smoked mackerel fillets, flaked
snipped chives, to garnish

1. Cook the pasta in boiling salted water for
10-12 minutes, or until just tender. Drain well.

Cook the courgettes in boiling salted water for
2-3 minutes until just tender.
2. Meanwhile, grate the rind of the oranges and
reserve. Using a serrated knife, peel and
segment the oranges, holding over a bowl to
catch the juice.
3. Whisk together the oil, orange rind and
juice. Season well and stir in the cooked pasta;
cool.
4. Combine all the ingredients with the flaked
mackerel, adjust seasoning and garnish with
snipped chives.

VARIATION You could also use canned
salmon, tuna or sardines, or smoked trout – just
keep the quantities the same.

Smoked Mackerel and Pasta Salad

WARM PASTA SALAD

SERVES 4

335 g (12 oz) dried pasta twists
salt and freshly ground black pepper
1 red pepper, seeded and chopped
1 green pepper, seeded and chopped
200 g can tuna steaks in brine, drained
3 × 15 ml tbs natural yogurt
green salad with a squeeze of lemon juice, to serve

1. Cook the pasta in boiling salted water for
10-12 minutes, or until just tender. Drain well.
2. Place the warm pasta in a serving dish and
stir in the chopped peppers, flaked tuna and
yogurt. Season to taste with plenty of pepper.
3. Serve immediately with a green salad,
sharpened with a squeeze of lemon juice.

PASTA AND PRAWN SALAD

SERVES 6

175 g (6 oz) dried pasta shells
salt and freshly ground black pepper
150 ml (5 fl oz) unsweetened apple juice
1 × 5 ml tsp chopped fresh mint
1 × 5 ml tsp white wine vinegar
225 g (8 oz) crisp eating apples
225 g (8 oz) cooked peeled prawns
shredded lettuce leaves, to serve
paprika, to garnish

1. Cook the pasta in boiling salted water for
10-12 minutes, or until just tender. Drain well.
2. Whisk together the apple juice, mint,
vinegar and salt and pepper to taste.
3. Cover and slice the apples. Stir the prawns,
apples and pasta into the dressing until well
mixed. Cover and refrigerate for 2-3 hours.
4. Before serving, add the shredded lettuce and
toss well. Divide between six plates and dust
with paprika to serve.

PASTA AND ANCHOVY SALAD WITH GARLIC DRESSING

SERVES 4

2 × 50 g cans anchovies in oil, drained
3 × 15 ml tbs milk
335 g (12 oz) small dried pasta shapes
salt and freshly ground black pepper
1 garlic clove, skinned and roughly chopped
3 × 15 ml tbs olive oil
juice of ½ lemon
1 red pepper, seeded and cut into thin strips
4 × 15 ml tbs mayonnaise

1. Place the anchovies in a bowl and add the
milk. Leave to soak for 30 minutes to remove
excess salt.
2. Meanwhile, cook the pasta in boiling salted
water for 10-12 minutes, or until just tender.
Drain well.
3. Drain the anchovies again and rinse under
cold running water. Pat dry with absorbent
kitchen paper.
4. Reserve a few of the anchovies whole for
garnishing and pound the remainder to a paste
with the garlic. Add the oil and lemon juice
gradually, whisking with a fork until thick.
Add pepper to taste.
5. Place the pasta in a large bowl. Pour in the
dressing immediately and toss well to mix.
Leave to cool, then cover and chill for at least
2 hours, or overnight if more convenient.
6. Add the red pepper strips to the pasta salad,
reserving a few for garnish. Add the
mayonnaise and toss gently to mix. Taste and
adjust seasoning.
7. Pile the salad into a serving bowl and arrange
the remaining whole anchovies and red pepper
strips in a lattice pattern over the top. Serve at
room temperature.

Pasta and Prawn Salad